EMMAUS BIBLE RESOURCES

Christ our Life

COLOSSIANS

EMMAUS BIBLE RESOURCES

Other titles available in the series:

A Rebellious Prophet – Jonah

Joy Tetley

Missionary Journeys, Missionary Church – Acts 13 – 20

Steven Croft

The Lord is Risen! – Luke 24

Steven Croft

EMMAUS BIBLE RESOURCES

Christ our Life

COLOSSIANS

DAVID DAY

Church House Publishing
Church House
Great Smith Street
London SW1P 3NZ

ISBN 978-0-7151-4352-0

Published 2003 by Church House Publishing

Copyright © David Day 2003

The right of David Day to be identified as the author of this work has been asserted by him in accordance with the Copyright, Designs and Patents Act 1988.

All rights reserved. No part of this publication may be reproduced or stored or transmitted by any means or in any form, electronic or mechanical, including photocopying, recording, or any information storage and retrieval system without written permission which should be sought from the Copyright Administrator, Church House Publishing, Church House, Great Smith Street, London SW1P 3NZ
Tel: 020 7898 1594
Fax: 020 7898 1449
Email: copyright@c-of-e.org.uk).

Cover design by Church House Publishing

Typeset in Franklin Gothic and Sabon

Printed in England by The Cromwell Press Ltd, Trowbridge, Wiltshire

Contents

How to use this book		vii
Introduction to **Emmaus Bible Resources**		ix
Acknowledgements		xi
An Introduction to Colossians		1

Chapter 1	**Plenty to Shout About – Colossians 1.1-20**	
	Dear Colossians – Colossians 1.1-2	9
	A lot to be thankful for – Colossians 1.3-5a	11
	The power of the good news – Colossians 1.5b-8	13
	A future full of possibilities – Colossians 1.9-14	16
	Christ who holds everything together – Colossians 1.15-17	18
	Christ first in the new creation – Colossians 1.18-20	20
	Guidelines for groups (1)	23
Chapter 2	**Someone to Watch Over You – Colossians 1.21–2.5**	
	The Main Thing – Colossians 1.21-22	26
	Keeping on keeping on – Colossians 1.23	28
	The cost of caring – Colossians 1.24	31
	Making it plain – Colossians 1.25-28	33
	An exhausting business – Colossians 1.29–2.3	36
	Keeping an eye on things – Colossians 2.4-5	39
	Guidelines for groups (2)	41
Chapter 3	**Reality and Shadows – Colossians 2.6-23**	
	Going back to square one – Colossians 2.6-8	45
	The basic principles of this world – Colossians 2.8	46
	Christ the conqueror – Colossians 2.9-13	49
	Nailing the accusation – Colossians 2.13-14	51
	Celebrating the triumph – Colossians 2.15	53
	Enjoying the freedom – Colossians 2.16-23	55
	Guidelines for groups (3)	58

Chapter 4   Christ in Everything – Colossians 3.1 – 4.1

Living in pictures – Colossians 3.1-4	60
Living in community – Colossians 3.5-17	62
Living in community (continued)	64
Living in households – Colossians 3.18 – 4.1	67
Living in households (continued)	69
Living in households (continued)	70
Guidelines for groups (4)	73

Chapter 5   Talking for the Kingdom – Colossians 4.2-18

Being a missionary congregation – Colossians 4.2-6	75
Being a missionary congregation (continued)	77
Nympha's diary	80
Paul's picture gallery of saints – Colossians 4.7-18	82
Paul's picture gallery of saints (continued)	85
Paul's picture gallery of saints (continued)	87
Guidelines for groups (5)	90

Liturgical Resources   93

Notes   98

Further Reading   99

Notes on the Order for Daily Prayer   101

An Order for Daily Prayer   102

How to use this book

The *Emmaus Bible Resources* can be used on your own, with a small group and with a whole church or group of churches (or any combination of the three).

On your own

Each chapter is divided into six parts ending with a short prayer or meditation.

You can use the studies as part of a daily time of Bible reading and prayer.

Or you can read the chapter with the biblical text at a single sitting.

A simple Order for Daily Prayer is provided at the back of the book.

With a small group

The group can be three friends, a husband and wife, an ongoing home group or one drawn together for these studies.

Each member of the group should read a chapter of this book and the biblical text between meetings.

At the end of each chapter, you will find a 'Guideline for groups' section.

Each group will need a convenor to guide you through this material.

With the whole church

The material is designed so that a church or group of churches could use it as the basis of Sunday and midweek material for learning and discussion.

How to use this book

A group of Sundays can be identified as appropriate for a series of sermons on Colossians. Tables of readings and other resources are provided in the Liturgical Resources section at the end of the book.

Members of the congregation who wish to engage with the text for themselves can then be encouraged to read this book as a study guide alongside the sermon series. Those who wish to do so can also meet in small groups during the week.

Overview of Emmaus Bible Resources		
Individual usage	**Small group usage**	**Whole church usage**
The book can form the basis of a daily time of reading and prayer.	Each chapter can be used as a 90-minute study.	A short series of sermons is envisaged, one for each chapter.

Guidelines
- To help the group dynamics – so that they understand each other and the biblical text better;
- For discussion questions – in order to assist reflection and application;
- For practical 'follow-on' activities that arise from each study.

Liturgical Resources
This section suggests ways of incorporating the study material into the ministry of the word as the congregation gathers on Sundays or during the week.
There is also an order for Daily Prayer.

Introduction to *Emmaus Bible Resources*

The two disciples walk along the road to Emmaus with Jesus, although they do not recognize him. As they walk together, Jesus interprets and opens the Scriptures to them. They have no books or texts with them but these disciples would already be familiar with many of the words of Scripture and would perhaps have learned them by heart.

From the earliest times, Christians have read the Scriptures on their own, together and in the company of the risen Christ. Every act of Christian worship has at its centre the public reading of the Bible, the word of God. Through reading and study of the Scriptures, our Christian faith is refreshed, strengthened, challenged and renewed. As Paul writes to Timothy:

> All scripture is inspired by God and is useful for
> teaching, for reproof, for correction, and for training
> in righteousness, so that everyone who belongs to
> God may be proficient, equipped for every good work
> (2 Timothy 3.16-17).

It is becoming harder to live as a Christian. Every Christian needs to live out the truth of their baptism: each one of us is called to Christian discipleship and Christian service according to the gifts God has given to us.

The *Emmaus Bible Resources* are offered as a way of encouraging individuals, small groups and congregations to engage with the text of Scripture in order that they may be built up and grow in Christian life, faith and service.

As with *Emmaus: The Way of Faith*, we have tried to combine sound and orthodox Christian theology with good educational practice on the one hand and a commitment to equip the whole Church for mission on the other.

Each book in the series is complete in itself and is intended as a guide either to a passage of Scripture or to a short series of passages grouped around a central theme. We hope to publish two or three books in the series each year. Normally the passage will be part of a longer book within the Bible, or it may be the whole of one of the shorter books.

Introduction to Emmaus Bible Resources

Each book in the series is largely written by one person (whose name appears on the cover) but has been edited by the original group of authors. We hope, over time, to involve others outside the original group in developing new material for the series.

Each author has been asked to write for a general Christian audience but to bring to the work insights from the Christian tradition of interpretation and the best of contemporary biblical scholarship. Notes and references have been kept to a minimum although there are some ideas for further reading. Each book also encourages a variety of learning styles in terms of individual study and reflection and group interaction.

Wherever possible, some of the material in each book has been piloted both with individuals and in small groups. We are very grateful to the churches, groups and individuals who have assisted in this way. The new series can be used just as well by individuals and churches who have not used the original *Emmaus* material as by those who have been using it for many years.

Five years after the publication of *Emmaus: The Way of Faith*, we are surprised and humbled at the many ways God has used the material, through the ministry and prayers of many Christian people and for the building up of Christians, of churches and, ultimately we pray, of the kingdom of God. Our prayer for this new series is that it may be used by God in similar ways and to the same ends.

Stephen Cottrell
Steven Croft
John Finney
Felicity Lawson
Robert Warren

Acknowledgements

I am grateful to everyone who read and reread this material, made suggestions and criticisms, expressed puzzlement, pulled faces, defaced drafts and patiently waited while I argued. In the end I have to admit that, in nearly every case, they were right and I was wrong. Six people read the whole manuscript and my debt to them is almost beyond words – almost but not quite. True to Paul's practice I can at least name them: Walter Moberly, the Rt Revd John Pritchard and Wendy Pritchard, Catherine Byrom, Steven Croft and Rosemary Day.

In addition I'd like to thank those congregations which heard most or part of the material in addresses at church house parties. I'm grateful for the feedback they gave me. So blessings on the assorted saints at South Parade Baptist Church, Leeds, and the churches of St Mary Bredin, Canterbury, St Michael, Paris and St George with St Martin, Poynton. Finally, thank you to those women's study groups at St Nicholas, Durham who tested the material in their characteristically vigorous and robust way and especially to Caroline Boardman for her comments on St Paul and checklists.

The publisher gratefully acknowledges permission to reproduce copyright material in this book. Every effort has been made to trace and contact copyright holders. If there are any inadvertent omissions, we apologize to those concerned and undertake to include suitable acknowledgements in all future editions.

Unless otherwise indicated, the prayers and reflections at the end of each section of text are by the author.

Bible quotations are from the *New Revised Standard Version of the Bible* copyright © 1989 by the Division of Christian Education of the National Council of the Churches in the USA. All rights reserved.

Extracts from *Common Worship: Services and Prayers for the Church of England* (Church House Publishing, 2000) are copyright © The Archbishops' Council of the Church of England.

The idea of a Faith Journal is taken from *Pew Rights,* by Roger van Harn, published by Wm. B. Eerdmans Publishing Co., Grand Rapids, Michigan, 1992, p. 155. Reproduced by permission.

Acknowledgements

The quotation from Sheila Cassidy is taken from *Sharing the Darkness*, published by Darton, Longman & Todd Ltd, 89 Lillie Road, London SW6 1UD, 1988, and is reproduced by permission.

An Introduction to Colossians

The letter to the Colossians wasn't written to us. When we read it we're looking over someone else's shoulder. Normally when we receive a letter we know the answers to the basic questions: Who is it from? Who is it written to? Why have they written it? Is it just full of newsy bits or is there a serious purpose? When we come to Colossians we have to read between the lines.

Scholars have relatively little to go on when they try to answer these questions. They search the letter for clues, try to link it to other parts of the New Testament and guess why it was written. But, in the end, they have no statement from on high that will settle all arguments.

Fortunately, this doesn't stop us reading Colossians for ourselves and learning from it, though if we can fill in something of the background the letter will make more sense. In what follows I have felt free to ignore the enormous range of different theories, in order to set out one possible reconstruction of the context of the letter. If you want to pursue the matter further then the commentaries mentioned at the end of this book all carry detailed discussions. Alternatively, you might like to construct your own theory based on careful reading of Colossians (along with Philemon, which is clearly closely connected with it).

Who wrote the letter?

The opening verse says that it comes from Paul and Timothy, and this was universally accepted until 1838. Since then some scholars have queried Pauline authorship but I am satisfied with the arguments supporting the traditional line.

Where was it written from?

Colossians itself states that Paul is in prison (4.10, 18 and perhaps 1.24), but does not tell us where. There are two main candidates – Rome and Ephesus – and, of the two, I have opted for Ephesus (despite the good case that can be made out for Rome). Rome was at least 1,200 miles away from Colossae, Ephesus only 100. When I try to make sense of Paul's personal comments in Colossians and the letter to Philemon, I can reconstruct the situation more convincingly if Paul was only just down the valley, rather than over a thousand miles away.

When was it written?

Nothing much hangs on the answer to this question but, if Paul is in prison in Ephesus, then the letter will need to be placed at some point during his ministry in that city. It's worth reading Acts 19 to catch the flavour of his time there, though that chapter gives only a selection of his triumphs and trials over a three-year period. Acts doesn't actually mention prison but maybe Paul has that in mind when he says that he 'fought with wild animals at Ephesus' (1 Corinthians 15.32) or refers to 'the affliction we experienced in Asia' (2 Corinthians 1.8). A likely date for the letter on this reconstruction would be in the mid-fifties, between AD 52 and 57.

Who were the Colossians?

Obviously, they were a group of Christians, meeting for worship in households (Colossians 4.13-15) but keeping close contact with one another and with Christians in the nearby towns of Laodicea (about ten miles away) and Hierapolis (about twelve miles away). Interestingly, Paul had never met the Colossians (2.1); the churches seem to have been born out of the evangelistic work of Epaphras, a native of the area and a companion of Paul. If Paul set up his base in Ephesus it is not too far-fetched to imagine that part of his strategy for the region involved his co-workers carrying the gospel from Ephesus on the coast down the valley into the interior (1.7). The church clearly contained men and women, parents and children and masters and slaves. It must, therefore, have included both well-to-do and poor. We cannot tell what the balance was but a disproportionate number of verses are devoted to advice to slaves and this may give us a hint (3.22-25). The vocabulary of the letter suggests that the church was made up primarily of Gentiles, though, since Colossae contained a large Jewish population, there may have been some Jews in the congregation as well.

Where is Colossae?

Colossae was in the Roman province of Asia, that is, modern Turkey. If you have been on holiday to Turkey you are sure to know Ephesus. This was Paul's base for three years. Moving inland from Ephesus up the river valley, you come eventually to Laodicea, Hierapolis and Colossae. These three towns formed a triangle in the valley of the River Lycus, just as it ran into the river Meander, and lay on the main West–East road across Asia. Colossae had known great prosperity, hardly surprising, considering the traffic between Ephesus and the interior. At the time the letter was written, however, it had lost something of its power and influence to Laodicea. A little later (in AD 60–61) earthquakes devastated the region, Colossae never recovered and the site has never been excavated.

From one viewpoint, then, Colossae was possibly the least important church to which Paul wrote. The modern tourist usually fastens on Ephesus with its magnificent theatre. You have to make an effort to take the coach into the interior and it's a 100-mile trip to Pammukale, famous for its hot springs. This is the site of Hierapolis. When we went there on holiday, I remember swimming in gloriously warm water and bumping gently into submerged Roman columns. On the journey back the guide waved airily out of the window at a mound of brown earth in the distance. 'That's Colossae,' he said and we drove on. I guess that St Paul would have smiled at this. He told the Colossians, 'your hope is laid up for you in heaven' – not in guide books and holiday brochures.

Why was the letter written?

This is the really important question, but that doesn't mean it is easy to answer. One scholar has identified 44 different theories about the situation that prompted Paul to write. We are unlikely to solve the matter in a paragraph or two! However, one thing is clear: Paul writes to warn the Christians against false teaching, which might seem attractive and might even lure them away from Christ.

Were the false teachers actually members of the church? This doesn't seem likely. Paul's tone is measured rather than angry (when Paul is angry he comes through loud and clear – try reading Galatians). He clearly thinks the Colossians are doing rather well in their spiritual journey (1.3-5; 2.5). This suggests that the false teaching was part of the air the Colossians breathed, a package of exciting ideas circulating in the marketplace or the baths, rather than heresy in the congregation.

Using our imagination (and, to be honest, going beyond the evidence) perhaps Epaphras brought a report to Paul about the alternative spiritualities in Colossae, admitting that he wasn't sure how to counteract them (apart from praying very hard: see 4.12). In response, Paul wrote a steadying and encouraging letter.

Unfortunately, Paul nowhere sets out in a systematic way what the false philosophy stood for. We have to read between the lines. The key verses for anyone who wants to have a go at understanding what was going on at Colossae are found in 2.8-23. What tentative conclusions can we draw from them?

> The words 'circumcised' and 'sabbaths' only make sense if the false philosophy had something to do with Judaism. 'Do not handle, do not taste, do not touch' along with 'food or drink' sound like kosher laws. So far so good.

> There are some strange phrases that are less clear: 'self-abasement', 'self-imposed piety, humility and severe treatment of the body' sound like mortification of the flesh. 'Worship of angels, dwelling on visions' point towards mystical experience.

> Then there are references to 'thrones or dominions or rulers or powers' and 'authorities' (1.16; 2.15) and the mysterious phrase 'elemental spirits of the universe' (2.8,20). I shall say more about these in Chapter 3 of this book.

So what was going on? Paul and his readers knew what he was talking about but we are in the dark. Nevertheless, I'll hazard a guess. We know that Colossae contained a large Jewish population. At the same time we also know that the steaming cities of the East provided a soil where all kinds of religions and philosophies could grow. In this hothouse of ideas it was easy to top up your own religion with a variety of pick 'n' mix beliefs. Is this what we have at Colossae? Confident Jewish teachers, thoroughly at home in Colossian culture, were trying to persuade the new converts that Christianity was only a halfway resting place. They urged them to go on to something better. The 'better' would entail strict observance of Jewish rules but the prize on offer was a mystical high that would take them into ecstatic worship with the angelic hosts.

At the same time the Colossians were living in a culture full of different 'Lords' who made absolute claims on their allegiance, a society of 'rulers, thrones, dominions and powers', which moulded people's lives and forced into their own image those who were too weak to resist.

It may seem as if this situation is far removed from anything we experience today but I think we do have parallels in our society. I went into my local bookshop and looked at the 'Mind, Body, Spirit' section, and the shelves on 'Health' and 'Management'. What struck me forcibly was the number of books offering to change people's lives for them. There were books on feng shui and your living room, on releasing your inner potential by a detox regime and on making a million in a year. Another shelf offered personal growth though meditation, tips on reading the tarot, the I Ching and the 'Book of Bones'. Further on I found books that would teach me how to dominate meetings, 'Know How People Think' and find fulfilment in tantric sex. A slim volume on spells for teenage girls offered me 'Health, Wealth, Beauty, Brains' – and 'Revenge'.

There is a pattern about all these books. On the one hand, the authors claim to have discovered something fundamental about the nature of humanity and the universe and state confidently, 'This is the way'. On the other, they offer something that is infinitely desirable and worthwhile – 'This is the prize'. 'This is the way and this is the prize' is not unlike the message the Colossian Christians were hearing. As we read Paul's response to the alternative lifestyles of the city, we may well learn truths that will help us as we try to follow Christ faithfully in our world.

The shape of this book

No letter in the New Testament gives such an exalted place to Christ. He is said to be the icon of the invisible God, the head of the Church, the Christian's life and hope of glory. He is Lord, the one who shall have first place in everything. This book aims to reflect this emphasis. Paul is addressing a specific problem; his answer is to show that, in Christ, the Colossian church can find everything it needs. As he develops his argument he peppers the letter with brilliant word pictures, vivid images that fire our imaginations. Some of these images may have gone stale on us and others may be hidden in the argument but it's worth watching out for them and allowing them time to stretch our minds and touch our hearts.

Chapter 1: Plenty to Shout About (1.1-20) looks at the different ways in which Paul encourages the church. He thanks God for his work in their lives, reminds them that the good news about Christ is unbelievably powerful and assures them of his confidence that God will go on working in them – in fact, he is praying that this will happen. Then he sets out what is virtually a hymn in praise of Christ. It's as if Paul is saying, 'Before I get on to the problem I want you to realize that the almighty God is at work in you and has given you everything you need in this incomparable Christ.'

Chapter 2: Someone to Watch Over You (1.21 – 2.5) lays bare Paul's heart. More than anything else God wants his Church to be holy and pure. This is 'the main thing' and Paul has spent his life concentrating on it. He exposes what that means in personal terms. Since he is totally committed to their growth into maturity, he urges the Colossian Christians to stand firm, suffers for them, teaches them, toils and labours on their behalf and watches over them. The strategy of this section of the letter is a sound one. Paul wants them to know that he will exhaust himself physically and spiritually for them. The argument runs: here is someone who cares; listen to what he says. He has earned the right to be heard.

Chapter 3: Reality and Shadows (2.6-23) is the heart of the letter. For the first time Paul refers to the dangers threatening the church. His focus is on Christ, however. All the fullness of God is in Christ, and 'in him' or 'with him' the Colossians experience his death and resurrection in their own lives. This means that in Christ they enjoy forgiveness of sins and freedom from any kind of condemnation. In him they can know victory over the powers that threaten to oppress them. In him they can face those who try to condemn them for failing to keep regulations (which are of human origin only) or disparage their Christian faith in the name of some allegedly superior mystical experience.

Chapter 4: Christ in Everything (3.1 – 4.1) looks at the life, individual and corporate, that should characterize Christians who set their minds on the exalted Christ. Paul lists the marks of the new humanity, a community that gives where the world grabs, builds up where the world puts down and brings together where the world splits apart. He then turns to the Christian household. In a context where power is unequally distributed he sets out key principles for handling both power and weakness.

Chapter 5: Talking for the Kingdom (4.2-18) begins with advice for living in society. It is interesting to see how much of this chapter emphasizes the importance of how we use words, whether in prayer, personal witness or affirmation. Paul urges the Colossians to pray, being watchful and thankful as they do so. He asks them to pray for him in his imprisonment that a door may be opened for the gospel. Then he exhorts them to behave sensibly towards non-Christians, making the most of the opportunities God sends and graciously commending the gospel. The letter ends with news of Paul's fellow workers and warm personal greetings and instructions.

Colossians contains only 95 verses. It can be read in 15 minutes. It would be helpful before you begin to get into this book to read the letter straight through with the above summary at your side. Read just to get the flavour and the sweep of the argument. Don't worry about details at this stage.

Blessed Lord,
who caused all holy Scriptures to be written
    for our learning:
help us so to hear them,
to read, mark, learn and inwardly digest them
that, through patience, and the comfort of your
    holy word,
we may embrace and for ever hold fast
    the hope of everlasting life,
which you have given us in our Saviour Jesus Christ,
who is alive and reigns with you,
in the unity of the Holy Spirit,
one God, now and for ever.

Common Worship: Collect for the Last Sunday after Trinity

Chapter 1
Plenty to Shout About – Colossians 1.1-20

Dear Colossians – Colossians 1.1-2

Colossae is a long way away when you are in prison, stuck there and unable to get out. If Paul was imprisoned in Ephesus, then we can imagine him looking in his imagination down the valley towards the interior. Over 100 miles away the little church meets Sunday by Sunday. Gazing out of the window, Paul can feel the breeze on his face. More than almost anything else he wants to be with them, to see how they are getting on. Are they standing firm? Are they faithful and resolute? Are there dangers to be avoided? False teachings to be resisted? The letter reveals something of the pain of separation, the frustration of not being able to be with the church in person and the anxiety of a father for his spiritual children. The news from Epaphras (see 1.8) had been encouraging but even that could not compensate for enforced absence. Halfway through the letter he will speak about being 'absent in body, yet . . . with you in spirit' (2.5). Almost his last words in this letter will be the poignant request, 'Remember my chains' (4.18).

But how to begin? Paul knows very well that the church at Colossae is set in a big city where lots of exciting ideas are buzzing about. Unfortunately, some of these ideas are opposed to the Christian faith and, if the Christians take them on board, then the little community will soon founder. The first few paragraphs of the letter will need to be carefully angled, therefore. Get them wrong and the hearers may not take him seriously or become deeply discouraged or go off in a huff.

In such circumstances, when the stakes are high and you are under stress, it is very easy to launch into a lament about how bad things are, how serious the danger and how likely the disaster, and end up leaving everyone considerably more miserable than when you started. Preachers are particularly prone to become preachy. They browbeat their listeners, majoring on sins, working out their pet dislikes and haranguing the congregation into sullen submission. For example, a sermon on 'Blessed are those who hunger and thirst after righteousness' needs to take account of the fact that a blessing is a blessing. You're supposed to feel good after hearing it. Yes, it's a challenge as well, but it would be a pity if the sermon did nothing but beat up the listeners because 'you lot don't hunger and thirst after righteousness'.

Preachers sometimes justify their bad temper by saying that people need to be confronted with the facts. Interestingly, that is exactly how Paul begins. He confronts the Colossians with the facts. But the great fact, the bedrock on which everything stands, is the reality of God's power and grace. And so his first words are about grace. There may be trouble ahead but it would be difficult to catch even a whisper of it before chapter 2, verse 4. Paul chooses to begin with the great realities: 'God is good, he is powerful, he is gracious and generous, he is at work in your lives and will go on working until you die – and as for Jesus! Now you're talking! Just let me go into overdrive about Jesus!' This is the pattern of the opening chapter.

Begin with grace. It's a good principle. It is easy to do the opposite. I seem to have spent a good deal of time in meetings that bewail the state of the Church. The English church attendance figures show a Church bleeding to death. Only 5 per cent of twenty-year-olds go to church. In one survey, only 28 per cent knew the gifts brought by the Wise Men, while 64 per cent knew that the TV detective who drives a red Jaguar is called Morse. After a decade of evangelism the membership of the Church of England has gone down, however you count the figures. Churches are boarded up or sold for mosques or warehouses or second-hand car salesrooms. And so on and so on and so on. I expect you recognize the tone.

Begin with grace. This letter begins by looking at the great facts of God's power and love. Of course, at the right time we will need to look realistically at the problems – but start with grace. In our own lives, in our church discussions and projects, in our sermons and home group studies, begin with grace.

This is why Paul begins with a God framework into which everything else can be fitted. He writes that this letter comes from Paul, an apostle by the will of God. That is, Paul is not some fanatical proselytizer desperately trying to make converts in order to make himself feel significant but God's messenger to them, entrusted with the truth about human life. Timothy is not an inadequate sidekick but a brother in the glorious work God has given them to do. The Colossians, brothers and sisters to each other and to Paul, are described as they are 'in Christ', that is, in God's eyes. When God looks at them he sees people who are 'holy and faithful', whatever they may feel about themselves on a rainy Monday morning. And so he wishes for them, not that they should have a nice day or 'take care' but that they would experience God's grace, his abundant love poured out on those who don't deserve it and are usually amazed and overwhelmed when they experience it. It's not surprising that those who are flooded with the love of God also experience Peace, the Old Testament blessing of *Shalom* – an untranslatable word that includes inner peace, wholeness of life, good relationships, a sure hope and strong personal foundations. The process of caring for those God has laid on his heart begins by setting them within this large framework. It would be a good start for us to see ourselves, our friends and family in the same perspective and wish for them the same blessings.

> God of grace and wholeness,
> thank you for those people you have given me to love,
> the saints, the faithful ones, my brothers and sisters,
>   especially . . .
> Help me to see the miracles you work daily in their
>   lives,
> and the surprises that are possible through your Spirit.
> Keep me from meddling or wanting to mould them in
>   my image,
> and touch their lives with your generosity and peace,
> through Christ our Lord. Amen.

A lot to be thankful for – Colossians 1.3-5a

If you want to cheer someone up it's not a good scheme to begin by criticizing them. Paul does not begin with, 'Let me point out a number of your faults. After that, I'll move on to an analysis of the mistakes you've made in the past. Then you'll feel better!' He begins by telling the Colossians that he thanks God for them every time he mentions them in his prayers.

Something interesting and powerful happens when we thank God for someone. Instead of assessing them according to our own set of values and ideas, we are led to look for evidence of God at work in their lives. Aspects of their character that we might never have noticed suddenly come to the fore. Thanking God presupposes that he has been busy in them, shaping them little by little to be more like Christ. At the very least it will mean that we are less inclined to despise them, criticize them or write them off. We might also be less disposed to 'improve' them. After all, the master painter has been at work on his masterpiece. Who are we to start putting our pathetic daubs here and there on his canvas?

Think of someone you know well. Systematically list the things for which you can thank God. Work through their personal qualities, the ways in which they have touched your life, the conversations you've had with them. Use your imagination to discern what God is doing in their lives. Don't be afraid of speculating. Leap into the future and imagine what he might have achieved in them in a year or two. Continue to thank him for his masterpiece. In the letter to the Ephesians (2.10) Paul uses the word *poiema* to describe God's activity in people. It's connected with our word 'poem', and has been variously translated as 'handiwork', 'workmanship' or 'masterpiece'. Basically God has made them what they are. Recognize his work in them and thank him for it (and them).

Most of all, thanking God for someone helps us to shift the burden of anxiety a little. He has been at work in their lives. We can be confident that, having started his work in them, he wants to go on and complete it. So Paul thanks God for the Colossians and begins to feel that, even though he is a long way away yet their spiritual growth doesn't depend entirely on him.

Someone has written that one of the main dangers of Christian service is lapsing into 'functional atheism'. By this phrase they meant that we can say that we are dependent on God while continuing to behave as if it were all down to us. Thankfulness reminds us that all Christian care and service for others is only effective because God's Spirit is operating. Yes, God has made us responsible but, before we collapse under the burden, we need to hear God saying to us, 'Do you think you could leave the management of the universe to me for a few minutes?'

It's easy to forget something else at this point – because it's so obvious. We read in our Bibles that Paul thanked God for the Colossians and we receive this information as if the apostle had written it to us. But we only read these words because Paul *told* the Colossians that he was thanking God for them. What happens inside you when someone *tells you* that he or she is thanking God for you?

Here we suddenly catch sight of one of the most attractive facets of Paul's character – his willingness to affirm people. He could have thanked God privately but is at pains to let the Colossians in on the conversation. 'Do you have any idea of the fantastic things God has done and is doing in your lives? Why, the things I've heard about you!' I suspect that many people grinned sheepishly and straightened up a bit when they heard these words. Of course, it was God at work in them but it was still nice to know that Paul had heard of their faith in Christ. And someone had told him that they loved one another with genuine Christian love. And had then gone on to point out how both faith and love were solidly based on their hope of enjoying the riches of Christ's grace in an unimaginably wonderful life in heaven. 'Who told Paul all this?' they wondered. 'It must have been Epaphras. He must have gone back to Paul with a glowing report.'

I assume that none of this was flannel or soft soap. The effect on the Colossians must have been considerable. Paul's words reassured them of the reality of God's work in them, it convinced them that they were really making progress, it encouraged them to stand firm in their faith, continue in their love and hold on firmly to their hope. And all this because Paul chose to tell them about his prayers.

By contrast, think of those wonderful replies that parents come out with when they want to annoy their children. 'What's for tea?' says the child, naturally curious, and gets an answer along the lines of: 'Nothing for noses.' 'Them as asks, don't get.' 'Wait and see pie.' 'Kate and Sidney pie.' 'Snake and pygmy pie.' 'Bread and pullet.' For heaven's sake, why is it so awful to tell someone what they're going to get for their tea?

Adults have talked like this for generations and it doesn't matter much. But our reluctance to affirm people in the Church does enormous damage. Are we worried that they will become arrogant? Do we feel it will do them good to be kept in their place? Contrast the grudging concession that someone may have possibly just about got something right with Paul's generous exposing of his prayer life. 'In our prayers for you we always thank God . . . because we have heard of your faith . . . and . . . love you have . . . because of the hope laid up for you in heaven.' 'You are God's project and it's marvellous to see what a fantastic job he's making of you all.'

Loving Lord,
thank you for your grace made visible in the lives of
    those I care about;
for their faith in Christ,
their love for others
and their hope for the life to come.
Increase their faith;
deepen their love;
and strengthen their hope,
now and all their days. Amen.

The power of the good news – Colossians 1.5b-8

People are not always ecstatically delighted as they settle down to listen to a sermon. In fact one writer has said, 'Assume they would rather feed their children to crocodiles than listen to you.' It's a harsh comment but one supported by the countless jokes about preachers and sermons. Like this one: 'Our minister's sermons are like the peace of God. They never come to an end and they pass all understanding.' Ho, ho!

This view is markedly different from what Paul is saying here. You came to faith, he says, when you heard the gospel. Your faith, love and hope are all connected to the message you received. Paul knows that everything God has done and is doing in the church at Colossae began when someone told them the good news. It looks as if it might have been Epaphras who was the messenger in this particular case. Conscientiously and faithfully, this 'beloved minister' told the story to the best of his ability and then stood back to watch the amazing power of the word of God explode into people's lives.

God doesn't hard-wire his message into people's brains, nor does he declare himself in thirty-foot-high neon lights in the sky with the headline, 'Yes, I do exist. You'd better believe it.' He prefers to entrust his good news to his followers. Jesus gave us the responsibility (and the privilege) of publishing the story of what God has done. It's an amazing vote of confidence in what we can do with his help.

When we examine what Paul says about the gospel we can see why it's good news. It is 'the word of the truth'. It tells about 'the grace of God'. In a world of spin where packaging the message is often seen as more important than its contents, the plain word of truth should come as a refreshing breath of fresh air. Christianity competes, of course, in the marketplace of claims to the truth. The world's great religions claim to be the truth. The gurus of alternative faiths queue up to tell us how to get our lives together, how to reorder our dining rooms, acquire a body like a film star, ensure our investments make a million and conceal the effects of growing old. We are all subjected to a worldwide debate, where hundreds of voices clamour to win the argument. In such a situation the gospel may seem like the weakest link, about to be banished from the discussion. We shouldn't be too anxious, however. It was always so. In the Introduction to this book, I drew a parallel between Paul's world and the 'Body, Mind and Spirit' section of our high street booksellers. In Paul's day the world was a battleground of beliefs and wandering preachers constantly offered the customers the secrets of life and success. In the Acts of the Apostles, Paul was cordially invited to give a presentation to the Areopagus, a cross section of the chattering classes, who liked nothing better than to hear which world view was new on the block this week. He got his 15 minutes of fame and then most of them laughed him off the stage (Acts 17.32).

But Paul was not ashamed or diffident about the good news. His response was to go on preaching. If he was rejected in one place, for example in a synagogue, then he moved to a secular lecture hall. In the babble of competing voices Christianity won in the end. Why? In the opinion of T. R. Glover[1] it was because 'the Christians out-lived, out-thought and out-died' the opposition. They knew that they were handling a message which was the truth, if people would only listen to it. Paul's words in this passage are amazingly upbeat and confident. The gospel is powerful, he says. It's spreading throughout the world. Everywhere it goes it 'is bearing fruit and growing'. Sometimes we feel abashed at the apparent weakness of the Christian faith and our own unwillingness to speak about it. Everyone else seems so confident in what they believe, so many people are deeply hostile to Christianity (or at least to the Church), we're not sure we can answer the difficult questions people might put to us. And so we stay silent and hope the opportunity will go away. 'Evangelism', in Rebecca Manley Pippert's words, 'is something you shouldn't do to your dog.'[2]

But the one thing we mustn't do is give up passing on the good news. Paul said it produces fruit and is growing throughout the world. When, like Epaphras, we try to do our bit, we find that God is at work in our weak and faltering words. To our amazement we occasionally find that some people are more ready to hear the message than we suspected. And, sometimes, we discover, years after the event, that seed we thought fell on stony ground did, in fact, bear fruit. Paul's attitude challenges us: 'Do I believe that the gospel is true and that God is at work wherever it is preached? If I do, will I look for opportunities to share my faith with others?'

It is good news, after all. Paul said it was about the grace of God. Christians have sometimes been guilty of preaching the good news as if it were bad news – making out that it was all about keeping rules, which you couldn't manage anyway, or joining a rather forbidding club that would constantly demand your subscription. But it is about the grace of God. Grace is God's love poured out on those who do not deserve it. In a world where there's no such thing as a free lunch, the gospel speaks of a God who is generous, who doesn't know how to stop giving, who forgives freely and fills us with his life. How can we keep silent?

Loving Father,
forgive the times when I have been embarrassed by
    the gospel
or ashamed to bear the name of Christian.
Renew my love for your world,

> my confidence in your gospel's power
> and my willingness to commend it to others.
> Through Jesus Christ our Lord. Amen.

A future full of possibilities – Colossians 1.9-14

At verse 9 Paul launches into a description of what he is asking God for every time he prays for the Colossians. If *thanking* recognizes that God has been at work then *asking* assumes that God *will* be at work. The technical term for asking in prayer, 'intercession', recognizes that people are full of possibilities once God gets hold of them. Whatever did the Colossians feel when they heard that Paul was praying for them and, in fact, never stopped praying for them? Perhaps we should tell people much more that they are in our prayers and perhaps we should follow Paul's practice of telling them precisely what we're praying for.

Paul's prayer is instructive. Sometimes we pray very specific prayers – about Aunt Edna's bunion or a forthcoming interview. I was once in a meeting that prayed that a hamster, lost beneath the floorboards, would re-emerge. (It did, the following day.) Paul's prayer is not as specific as that but neither is it so vague as to come in the 'God bless everyone in the world' category. His prayer covers four areas of a Christian's life and focuses on spiritual growth and maturity rather than tiny detail. That doesn't mean it's vague or bland, however.

The first cluster of words has to do with 'knowing'. He asks that God will fill the Colossians with knowledge, spiritual wisdom and understanding. It is easy to see life from an entirely secular perspective. We rely on our intellect and our common sense. When confronted with a dilemma we may toss a coin or calculate the likely outcome or list pros and cons. Paul prays that Christians may learn to see life from God's perspective – in the light of eternity. God's way of doing things has often looked like folly from a worldly standpoint. God's values are unworkable, we may think. Forgiving your enemies, being generous to a fault, treating people as if they were made in his image 'doesn't work in the real world'. Paul is keen that this community in Colossae should see the world in the light of Christ – who points us towards the power of God in weakness and the wisdom of God in apparent foolishness. He prays that they may be open to receive this wisdom, obedient to follow it, willing to trust God even in the darkness, shaped by his way of doing things.

The second cluster is about 'doing'. Wisdom and understanding are not given just to amuse us. Verse 10 reminds the Colossians that knowledge is to be put to use in a practical way. 'That you may lead lives worthy of the Lord', 'pleasing to him', 'as you bear fruit in every good work'. This may sound a little stuffy. Does God really want an army of do-gooders? Well, I know that some good deeds are done out of duty or guilt or because the doer is a control freak. But I am actually quite proud to read that the percentage of churchgoers involved in voluntary work is 46 per cent, as against 17 per cent in the general population. And I'm impressed when I encounter a woman who, in a single day, threw a party for her grandchildren, bought her husband a trout for his tea 'because I knew he'd like it' and wheeled someone else's baby around in the pushchair so that the child's mother could get some sleep. That's the stuff of goodness and those on the receiving end are warmed, feel cared for and valued. I'm equally impressed when I hear of someone who resisted the temptation to cut corners at work or spoke up for a colleague who was the target of everyone else's bile. Paul picked out the key motive as 'pleasing the Lord' – not stroking your ego. This motive frees us to be spontaneous and creative in our good deeds. It also encourages the question: What have I done within the last 24 hours that has made God say, 'I'm really glad you did that!'? God grins when we are good.

The third group of words concerns 'standing firm'. Paul asks that they may be 'made strong with all the strength that comes from his glorious power'. Why? So that they might 'endure everything with patience'. The Christian life is a battle and Paul recognized that the Church would be under pressure. He prays that they will stand firm in difficult situations and not flinch. He also asks that they may put up with difficult people.

There are moments of risk when one's commitment is most fragile. Many of them are associated with a change of life circumstances – leaving home, going to college, the first job, the first child, the mid-life crisis, the last child leaving home, the departure of a trusted and well-loved minister, moving to a new area, friends moving away, being bereaved. In such situations we need to pray our friends through the difficult patch. We also need to know that someone is praying for us as we face these moments when our faith is under pressure. Paul prays that they will keep the faith and stand their ground. I was present once at a confirmation service when the bishop electrified the congregation by challenging the candidates. 'Will you be standing here next year?' Then he went on: 'And will you be here in five years' time? And if I should come tottering in on a Zimmer frame in twenty years' time, will you still be standing firm in the faith?'

The final cluster of words is about doing all this with joy and thanksgiving. The last paragraph may make the life of faith seem grim, an unrelenting battle against sin, the world and the devil. Joy and thanksgiving lift our spirits. Thanksgiving assumes public praise. Of course, we praise God inwardly in our prayers but Paul assumed that much of the praising would be done in the presence of others. Joy and thanksgiving cannot be manufactured. A fixed smile hurts your face after a while. Joy and thanksgiving are gifts from God. Paul prays that, as the Colossians meditate on what God has done for them – 'rescued from darkness', 'enabled to share in the inheritance of the saints in the light', 'transferred into the kingdom of his beloved Son', 'redemption', 'forgiveness' – then an unstoppable fountain of joy and thanksgiving would well up within them.

This is a comprehensive prayer. One way of using it would be to think of someone you know well and lay the four emphases over their life like a grid. Pray them into maturity. In God's presence see them receiving his wisdom at their prayers, walking about doing good, standing firm against pressure, giving thanks to God with a smile. And is there anyone who will pray like this for you?

> Almighty God,
> you long that we should grow into maturity in
>   the Spirit,
> pour upon us your good gifts:
> the gifts of wisdom and understanding,
> of goodness and service,
> of strength and endurance,
> of thanksgiving and joy.
> and form us in the likeness of Christ. Amen.

Christ who holds everything together – Colossians 1.15-17

If we set verses 12 to 20 to music we would get the sense that the volume was starting to increase somewhere around verse 13. The organ note swells, we become aware of complex harmonies, other instruments join the theme tune until suddenly the sound breaks forth into the triumphant affirmation, 'He is the image of the invisible God . . . !' We can understand how some commentators think Paul is making use of an early Christian hymn at this point.

Whether the passage is a hymn or not, the language certainly goes into overdrive. We want to know why Paul so dramatically changes the tone. What did he have in mind? After all, this early part of the letter is designed to encourage the Colossians and help them to stand firm. How do these poetic lines achieve that purpose?

A likely explanation is that Paul wants them to see the big picture. Up to this point the camera has been in close, focused on the Christians' personal and community life. The tiny details are sharply defined but the background remains blurred. Now the camera team is whisked up into the sky as if in a helicopter. We see the Colossians in their immediate context and then, in a second, we are so far above the earth that we almost lose sight of them as we catch a vision of the whole created universe.

And what a breathtaking picture Paul paints. He exults as he focuses on Christ. He is the image or icon of the God who is invisible. The icon is like a photo or the image on a coin. It's a representation of the real thing. Occasionally I visit an old lady of 92. On the top of the piano are dozens of photographs, lovingly dusted and displayed. 'That's our Jim,' she'll say. Or 'that's Kevin and Diana at their wedding'. Well, it isn't, of course. But it is a representation of them. As a result I think I have a pretty good idea of what Jim, Kevin and Diana look like. They're not just pictures either. Something of the real Jim, Kevin and Diana comes through the images, not least in the proud and tender way she handles the photographs. The icons on my computer illustrate this idea in a different way. I look at the little picture on the screen and I know that if I double click on it, I shall suddenly be taken right to the heart of my email facility. The icon is like a little doorway through which I can enter the reality to which it points.

You can't press illustrations and analogies too far, of course, but the concept of Christ as icon of the God you can't see is a powerful one. Archbishop Michael Ramsey once wrote: 'God is Christlike and in him there is no unChristlikeness at all.'[3] In Christ, walking, talking, acting, loving, dying, rising from the dead, we see a perfectly true reflection of Almighty God.

But now Paul is on a roll. This Christ, God's icon, must not be reduced just to the carpenter from Nazareth. He existed in the heart of God before anything was created. He is the power or agent through which everything was created – things you can see but also invisible spiritual powers and forces. This idea – that Christ was the agent through which spiritual forces came into being – is going to be used in a powerful way later in the letter. Hang on to it. So all things were created *by* him but also *for* him. And, playing a final ace, Paul says, 'And everything that exists now only goes on existing because he sustains it. *In him* all things hold together.'

Put very simplistically, this implies that Christ had a life before Bethlehem. The universe came into being through him. The Christmas carol says, 'we will rock you . . . darling, darling little man'. I have to say I prefer 'Lo! Within the manger lies, he who built the starry skies'.[4] It seems closer to the truth. Christ is the cosmic glue that holds everything together. Christ is the tune that gives shape and meaning to the jumble of assorted notes. Take away Christ and the universe collapses into nothingness. It isn't like pulling the plug out of the socket and complaining that the television won't work. Pull Christ out of the socket and you don't have a television set at all. As someone put it: 'Christ is the reason gloss paint glosses, grass is green, ducks quack and stars spin.' Even as the atheist declares, 'There is no God', it is because of Christ that his vocal cords hold together and allow him to utter the words.

Now, even though systematic theology has been written on the basis of these verses, we ought not to forget that they are primarily poetry. Paul gives us a picture of the cosmic, incomparable Christ. The picture is mind-blowing, breathtaking, heart stopping, blood tingling – but it was written so that it might also be *life changing*. Once I've got a glimpse of the sheer 'size' of Christ, the poetry is intended to lead me, not into speculation, but into adoration and praise.

Creator God,
by whose almighty word the heavens and the earth
    were formed
open our eyes to see
the majesty of your power,
the beauty of your universe
and the glory of Christ,
through him by whom all things were made
and in whom all things hold together. Amen

Christ first in the new creation – Colossians 1.18-20

In the space between verses 17 and 18 something goes horribly wrong. Paul doesn't spell it out but the words, 'from the dead', 'reconcile', 'making peace' and 'blood of his cross' indicate that not everything is perfect in this universe – and that's before we get to 'estranged', 'hostile' and 'evil deeds' in verse 21. The Creation is spoiled, fractured in some way. Instead of being in perfect harmony with God, human beings are at odds with him.

There are dozens of ways of portraying this. We can turn to the first chapters of the Bible and say that sin enters Paradise. That story ends with thorns, briars and the way back to the Garden barred by a fiery sword. Or we can use contemporary analogies – and speak of a virus in the depth structure of the computer which ensures that everything is marred and distorted in unpredictable ways. Paul began by showing us a picture of a universe that was totally, beautifully and delicately responsive to the will of God, like an ice-skating pair in perfect harmony. Suddenly we realize that the picture has changed – inside the universe as we experience it, there are elements that are hostile and contrary to that perfect will. One skater in the pair is determined to go his or her own way, regardless of the routine they had rehearsed. This spells disaster. It's like pulling out the vertical threads of a loom. If you persist, holes appear and eventually the cloth unravels.

What will God do in this crisis? One possible reaction is for him to bin the whole project. God looks at the mess, sighs wearily and returns to the drawing board. Put the first attempt down to experience and try again. Maybe he can come up with a more robust model the second time round. Most of us would think that was a reasonable response. And so it is if you are dealing with objects – cars, refrigerators, jam sponges and bookshelves. But perhaps we would think twice if the uncooperative raw material were members of our family – our children perhaps. Then we would be more likely to persist, to try any method we could think of, to twist and turn and be as creative as our imagination would let us, if only we could restore the harmony we once enjoyed.

Paul says that God decided to work from the inside. He begins a rescue operation to get his creation back. Jesus Christ is 'the fullness of God' appearing within this world, living a perfect human life – just as humanity was designed. Just once the Maker's instructions were followed to the letter, all the way from Bethlehem to Golgotha. Just once God and humanity were perfectly in tune. Christ is the beginning of a new humanity, in him a new kind of human being, a kind of Adam and Eve Version Two, enters the world.

He is the head of the body, the Church, the beginning and the firstborn of a new race of men and women. In every way you can think of, Jesus is supreme. Now, says Paul, those who follow Christ, who are grafted on to him are part of that new humanity. He is the head, no one can rival that, but like limbs and organs in a body, the Church is a community of people into whom and through whom Christ's life is flowing.

In these glorious verses we catch a glimpse of how Christ's life given up willingly on the cross, absorbed everything that humanity could throw at him. In Christ God soaked up the evil, the sin and the rebellion of an unruly universe and drew the poison out of it by letting it flow through him. We can understand this from human relationships. Since the hurts cannot be undone, absorbing the injury is the key to making up and restoring friendship. There isn't any other way to be reconciled with someone who is at odds with you. Something has to give or, better, someone has to give way and take the hurt and the injury into themselves in order to make clear space for the parties to come together again.

In a similar way, Paul argues that everything necessary has now been accomplished for the created world to come back into harmony with God, to return to the order for which it was created. In Christ God has reconciled everything to himself, in Christ God has made peace through the blood shed on the cross. This is why Christians make so much of Good Friday and why churches have crosses everywhere.

In a few verses Paul has taken his readers to the edge of space. On a vast canvas he paints a vision of the universe, made for God's glory and its own delight, and sustained by Christ every moment of its existence. We are taken up into the great dance of the spheres and see how creation was designed to praise God at the top of its voice. We also see that the world as we know it is flawed and that humanity is part of that deep tragedy. Then we are summoned to see God entering the disaster area in the person of Christ, 'the young Prince of Glory', taking all the rebellion into himself so that, somehow, he might have his creation back. We are on holy ground. This is the good news, which is being proclaimed all over the world and is growing and producing fruit (1.6). Our response is not to argue about details; it is to be lost in wonder, love and praise. 'Tell out, my soul, the greatness of the Lord.'

Almighty God,
who wonderfully created us in your own image
and yet more wonderfully restored us
through your Son Jesus Christ:
grant that, as he came to share in our humanity,
so we may share the life of his divinity;
who is alive and reigns with you,
in the unity of the Holy Spirit,
one God, now and for ever.

Common Worship: Collect for the First Sunday of Christmas

Guidelines for groups (1)

This section at the end of each chapter gives guidelines for a 90-minute meeting of a small Bible study group of up to a dozen people. You could also use the material as a guide for a much smaller group of two or three friends or family members (in which case the timings may be different). The guidelines assume that the group members have looked at the Bible passage before the meeting and, ideally, have read through at least some of the reflections in this chapter. In most of the sections I've provided more questions than any single group could manage at one time. I suggest that you choose, say, two questions from *Sharing together*, not more than three from *Studying together* and one each from *Praying together* and *Taking action together*. Alternatively, a group may decide to take much longer over the questions, spending three or four weeks over each chapter and pursuing questions in depth. The important thing is to choose what suits you best.

Clearly the section on *Taking action together* is likely to make considerable demands on the time of a group. It may be frustrating to chase through many projects at speed when a more thorough involvement in one would be more satisfying and useful. Many of the suggestions lend themselves to becoming 'mission projects' in the style described by Steve Croft in the book, *Transforming Communities*. For a full account see especially Part Four, 'Enabling Transforming Communities'.[5] A mission project of this kind would focus the study and concern of the group, would run through the whole period that this book is in use and might well continue long after the study of Colossians had finished.

Sharing together (20 mins)

1. If this is a new group meeting, on the first occasion all, in turn, should take a moment to introduce themselves.

2. Each member of the group should say something about their hopes for your meetings together to discuss Colossians. Ask everyone to give their initial impressions from reading Colossians 1.1-20 and the study material. If you can, share one thing you gained and one question you bring.

3. Talk about one occasion when you were affirmed. Describe what it felt like.

4. How easy is it to affirm others? And how easy is it to receive affirmation? What kinds of thing do we find affirming?

Studying together (50 mins)

1. Paul hopes for *peace* for the Colossians. He is thinking of the Old Testament word, *Shalom*. Give examples of what *Shalom* – wholeness – might mean for you, in terms of inner development, family relationships, your work, friendships, church life, hopes for the future.

2. 'Evangelism is something you shouldn't do to your dog.' Do you find speaking about faith difficult? If so, why might this be? How can we help one another to be more comfortable about sharing the gospel?

3. 'Once I've got a picture of the "sheer size" of Christ . . .' What helps you see the greatness of Christ? It might be a building, a hymn or song, a painting, a poem, a passage in a book. Share your experiences with the rest of the group.

4. 'We can't rejoice in what God has done, unless we first feel that there is a problem.' How would you describe the problem to which Christ is the answer?

5. 'Something has to give or, better, *someone* one has to give way and take the hurt and the injury into themselves in order to make clear space for the parties to come together again' (p.22). Can you think of specific situations where someone chooses to absorb hurt in order to work towards reconciliation?

Praying together (10 mins)

1. Much of this chapter is about thankfulness. Think of one other person who has touched your life. As you think of them, remember in God's presence the different things for which you are thankful.

2. Pray for a particular person, laying the four aspects of Paul's prayer (see 'A future full of possibilities', pp. 16–18) over their specific situation. What kind of *understanding and wisdom* do they need? Imagine them *doing good*. In what situations will they need to be able to *stand firm*? For what will they be especially *thankful*?

3. What have you done within the last week that has made God say, 'I'm really glad you did that'? Don't disparage the routine and mundane. Thank God for his grace at work within you.

Taking action together (10 mins)

The group may decide to work on one of the following projects during the week ahead.

1. Make a resolution to tell certain people that you thank God for them. Report back at the next meeting.

2. Design a leaflet suitable for giving to visitors to church, which sets out the good news in an interesting and relevant way. Suggest ideas for visual material as well as for text.

3. Collect materials for a time of worship, reflecting on what God has done through Christ in reconciling the world to himself.

Chapter 2
Someone to Watch Over You – Colossians 1.21–2.5

The Main Thing – Colossians 1.21-22

In the great hymn that ended the last section Paul has taken his readers into the furthest realms of the universe, far out beyond the stars. They've looked at 'all things, in heaven and on earth'. Therefore what comes next may have been something of a shock for them. Paul suddenly zooms down to earth and makes matters very personal. In the Greek in which the letter was written, the paragraph begins with two words.

'And you . . .'

'Where are you in all this?' Paul asks. 'Let me tell you. Within this canvas, even though it is vast, if you stop and look you will find yourself.' Just as people pore over a photograph of a big event – a football crowd or a pop concert or even an old school photograph – trying to pick themselves out, so he puts the Colossians inside the frame. We know the feeling. 'There I am,' we shriek. 'Look! Just to the right of the policeman!' Paul has suddenly made everything very personal – for the Colossians and for us. In a word, Christ died to make sure that *you* would be in the big picture.

These verses contain another couple of words that Paul is fond of using. After 'And you . . .', he puts the word 'once' and eleven words later follows up with 'now'. In a famous report on a football match David Coleman, the TV commentator, is supposed to have said, 'This was a game of two halves. . . .' Paul would have understood what he meant. '*Once* you were like this . . . but now you are like this.' The two words divide the two halves of his sentence but they also mark the two halves of the Colossians' story. 'Once you were . . . but now you are . . . .' They could have written a book about everything contained within those two key words.

As with every 'Before . . . After' advertisement, the 'Before' part is fairly uncomplimentary. Once you were alienated from God, says Paul. You and he were like strangers to each other. In fact, your way of seeing things was so opposed to his that you were his spiritual enemies. And your lifestyle and behaviour so out of harmony with him that they are best described as evil. And then you encountered Christ. Through his death he made it possible for you to be reconciled to God. As the communion prayer puts it: 'When we were still far off you met us in your Son and brought us home . . . .' God made a decisive move towards us, even when we were pretty content to go our own way.

Paul's words emphasize the physical nature of what Christ did. This act of reconciliation didn't consist of comforting words communicated from a throne in the sky. It involved flesh, thorns, blood, pain and a cry of despair. It was in 'his fleshly body through death', through arms stretched wide and pinned down tight, that the gulf was bridged and the new friendship established.

At this point Paul reveals the Main Thing about the Christian life. More than anything else, God wants a real relationship with us. It was this desire that brought Jesus to earth. Deepening and enriching the friendship was, and is still, God's major project. Now, Paul says, God is committed to making sure his plan is brought to completion.

When he describes the Main Thing, Paul uses picture language drawn from the worlds of the temple and the law court. First, he says that God wants to make us an offering, to make us into a kind of present for himself. His purpose is 'to present or offer us' like the offerings in the temple, making us 'holy', set apart or special, without any spot or blemish, just like the animals used in the temple rituals. Those animals were selected to die, of course, but God intends that we should enjoy abundant life. If we are going to be God's treat then we can expect him to lavish time and energy on us. Later in the sentence Paul uses a word usually translated 'irreproachable' or 'free from accusation', and this term is taken from the law courts. No one can criticize, pick holes or bring charges against us. God is fiercely committed to his friends. Someone once confessed to Cardinal Hume that they were put off by the idea that God was watching them all the time. 'But he is,' said the Cardinal. 'He loves us so much he can't take his eyes off us.'

Management consultants often say, 'The main thing is to make sure that we make the main thing the main thing.' The Main Thing about the Christian life is that it is that process by which God through Christ makes us into a perfect offering. God devotes his time to shaping us into the shape of Christ. He works in us to create, or perhaps better, to *recreate* a new humanity, humanity as we were intended to be. He wants us to become more and more like Christ, that is, more holy, more obedient and more loving. We sometimes think following Christ is about God making us happy. We forget that he wants to make us truly human. We ask for silver; he is desperate to give us gold. We want a quick MOT, a lick of paint and a bit of spit and polish; he will be satisfied with nothing less than a new creation. This is the Main Thing – and the cost to God is already incalculable. He is unlikely to pull out before the job is completed.

> Father of all,
> we give you thanks and praise,
> that when we were still far off
> you met us in your Son and brought us home.
> Dying and living, he declared your love,
> gave us grace, and opened the gate of glory.
> May we who share Christ's body live his risen life;
> we who drink his cup bring life to others;
> we whom the Spirit lights give light to the world.
> Keep us firm in the hope you have set before us,
> so we and all your children shall be free,
> and the whole earth live to praise your name;
> through Christ our Lord.
>
> *Common Worship*: Prayer after Communion,
> Holy Communion Order One

Keeping on keeping on – Colossians 1.23

Paul was a Christian minister and the rest of this week's readings take us more deeply into his mind. His theme is that of feeling responsible for other Christians. For him the burden was aggravated because he was far away from them and unable to be physically present to reassure or encourage. It's good to talk but email or the phone is no substitute for a face to face over a cup of coffee.

We may not be apostles but that doesn't mean we can't learn anything from one. So Paul prompts us to ask, 'For whom am I responsible?' And 'How are they doing?' Sometimes the responsibility is a formal one. A youth club leader agonizes over his or her group. School is a rough place in which to be a Christian: assemblies are places of trial rather than acts of worship. Will they stand firm? Will they grow in confidence and maturity? Meeting them once a week seems a fragile way of producing defenders of the faith. Will my prayers stop the waters bursting through the dam?

Parents worry over their children. Every Sunday morning produces the equivalent of World War III as the debate about going to church surfaces again. 'Do we have to go? It's boring. None of my friends go. There aren't any normal boys there. They're all nerds and anoraks.' At the back of the discussion lurk the questions, 'Will my children have faith? Will they grow up with strong convictions and solid values? Or will we be the last Christian generation in our family?'

And the converse is true. I've met many teenagers and students who are similarly anxious about their parents, who pray for them earnestly and want to see them come to faith.

Close to Paul's situation are those who have responsibility for members of a group, most commonly a home group associated with a church. One person is deeply depressed, a couple are going through a difficult time in their marriage, a young woman is trying to discern if she is being called to the ordained ministry, another person is in deep grief and anger against God because a friend committed suicide. Paul spoke elsewhere of 'the care of all the churches'. To try to care for a group of people can sometimes feel like juggling eight spinning plates, any three of which threaten to come crashing down at any moment.

These are just a few examples. I doubt if any of us does not have someone for whom we feel responsible. Perhaps I should put it in a different and even more terrifying way. God has made us responsible for some other person's spiritual health. If we take that duty seriously then we know from the inside something of what Paul felt like as his thoughts turned towards the little community at Colossae. Like him we want to fulfil our responsibilities properly. We long to see the other person grow up into Christ. Their growth in the faith is a concern that God has given us. It is part of our calling. In that sense, then, every Christian is a minister and is called to service in the church family. No one can say, 'I have no gifts; I can't do this.' If 'this' is caring for another Christian then we can all do 'this'. In fact, it is one of the most important tasks we can do for the kingdom of God. What can Paul's approach to the task teach us?

He begins by urging the members of the young church to remain firmly holding on to the faith. We recall the prayer earlier in the letter – that they might endure (1.11). 'You need to hang on,' says Paul. In the Church of England baptism service we pray that the person being baptized will 'remain faithful to Christ to the end of your life'. At the end of his life Paul will say, 'I have finished the race, I have kept the faith' (2 Timothy 4.7). There isn't much chance of becoming like Christ if we drift out of contact or actually refuse to keep the lines of communication open.

Verse 23 reminds the Colossians that the gospel is good news and powerful news. It has the potential to transform people's lives, to turn them upside down and inside out, to carry them over from death to life. But good news of God's friendship freely offered has still got to be accepted and lived in. It would be a strange friendship where one party never bothered to return letters, cards, phone calls, emails, never took up invitations to come round for a pizza or a video, never shared any news of what they'd been doing or showed any interest in what their friend had been up to, and never sent a card or a present for birthdays. At some point we would wonder if this 'friendship' could be called a friendship at all. If we remain in contact with God, he can do something with us. If we sit in a corner, seldom communicating and then only in surly grunts we can't complain if the friendship doesn't blossom and develop.

Paul saw himself as a servant of the good news. He wanted to cooperate with God in his ambitious project. And so, at the start of this section of the letter, he warns the Colossians against an easy-going complacency. 'Don't think you can come and go as you please. Don't presume on God's goodwill. Don't treat his kindness with contempt.' There's a seriousness and an urgency about Paul's words that may seem exaggerated in our culture. 'Oh come on,' we are inclined to say, 'cut us a bit of slack. It surely doesn't matter if we shop around a bit. Why take it all so seriously?' For Paul it was a matter of life and death.

I suppose one question that comes out of verse 23 is 'Do we care enough about the people for whom we are responsible to remind them about the seriousness of Christian commitment?' Exhortation is likely to be misunderstood as nagging. It may introduce a discordant note or seem to be undermining a relationship. But exhortation is also the mark of real caring. It's the kind of thing wives do for husbands, doctors for patients, teachers for pupils and parents for children. A friend told me about his experience as a teenager in the church. His minister helped him work out a simple 'Rule of Life', a written commitment that spelt out his resolutions about such things as praying, saying grace at meals and going to Communion. He said that, once it had been written down, he signed it and then it was offered up at the communion table at the next Eucharist. Many years later he still speaks about the impression this made on him. He had come to realize that being a Christian was more than grabbing all the freebies God had to give and then doing what you liked. His minister had impressed on him the seriousness of following Jesus. Paul exercised his responsibility as a servant of the gospel partly by emphasizing the importance of keeping on keeping on. 'Continue securely established and steadfast in the faith, without shifting from the hope promised by the gospel.'

Faithful God,
whose commitment to us never fails,
I pray for my brothers and sisters in Christ,
and for myself.
Keep us steadfast in faith,
never shifting from the hope we have in the gospel.
When life is easy, preserve us from complacency,
when it is hard, keep us from despair.
Give us grace to fight the good fight, finish the course
    and keep the faith;
through Christ, who, for our sake, was obedient even
    to the cross. Amen.

The cost of caring – Colossians 1.24

'I am now rejoicing in my sufferings for your sake, and in my flesh I am completing what is lacking in Christ's afflictions for the sake of his body, that is, the church.' At first sight this is an extraordinary and puzzling verse. Did Paul really dare to compare his sufferings with those of Christ? Is he setting himself alongside Jesus in the redemption of the world?

This explanation is very unlikely. It's hardly possible that the Paul who has just described Christ as the firstborn in all creation and the head of the Church would make such a comparison. He has just written that Christ 'might come to have first place in everything'. Paul would never put himself on the same level as Christ, in whom the fullness of God dwells. So what might he have meant?

One possible explanation is that Paul realized that this world is locked into a cycle of sin, pain, suffering, disease and death. That's the way it is and that's the way it will go on being until Christ comes in glory and brings in a new heaven and a new earth. Meanwhile we are all caught up in the vicious spiral. Jesus' life and death demonstrated that anyone who comes to do the will of God will experience in his or her own body the kind of world this is. Jesus was not immune from it and suffered at the hands of people who were a part of this broken world. So, Paul might be saying, Christ goes on suffering in his body – except that his body now is the body of the Church, that is, all Christians. Paul is imprisoned because he has chosen to follow Christ. As he is part of Christ's body Christ continues to suffer in him. And Paul thus continues to fill up in his flesh part of the sum total of sufferings that Christ will suffer in his followers until the end of time. The important point that Paul is making is that he is glad to be able to do this – for Christ – and also, in a strange way, for the Colossians. If Paul had refused to be a servant of the gospel he could have enjoyed a happy and trouble-free life – but then the Colossians would not have come to know Christ and the benefits of his death and resurrection.

There's a bit more to this as well. It isn't just that Paul's willingness to suffer was part of the price that had to be paid so that the Colossians could come to know Christ and grow up into him. Paul's experience was itself a sermon, it was part of the message. In an amazing and profound way, the Colossians could see the gospel pattern of death and life, of life coming out of death, woven into the flesh of Paul. Paul literally *embodied* the good news. As he says at the end of his letter to the Galatians, 'I carry the marks of Jesus branded on my body' (Galatians 6.17).

How can this have anything to say to us, who are involved in looking after people in an altogether less dramatic way? For most Christians in the West, caring for others in the church is not likely to lead to prison. In other parts of the world, alas, that kind of hardship remains a real possibility. But Paul's words still provoke us to ask about the personal cost of taking on responsibility for another Christian. Real care for someone else is never going to be without some kind of cost. Pastoral care may quite possibly involve pain.

Parents have known this for centuries, of course. The story may begin with carrying the child and the labour of giving birth, but it doesn't end there. It continues through getting up at 3 a.m., mopping up vomit (engagingly called posset or gloop), scrimping and saving, mending, washing and ironing, running a taxi service, giving up the use of your car, providing an instant audience for listening, applauding and appreciating, lying awake at nights worrying what time they're going to come in, agonizing over an unsuitable boy or girl friend, bankrolling their education, fashion whims, leisure pursuits and business ventures. 'Aren't they ever off your hands?' parents wail. The answer is 'Probably not.' This is what it takes to bring a baby to maturity, to be involved in the forming of a human being. The extraordinary thing is that most parents rejoice in the process.

In the same way people are not formed into the likeness of Christ without some cost. It may be spending time on Tuesday nights down at the youth centre when you could be doing something more interesting at home. It may be listening to someone in deep depression, finding yourself drained and exhausted by the process, and suspecting that next week you will be doing it all again. It may be faithfully running a house group year after year, and staying with people on their roller coaster ride of faith. It may be allowing yourself to be sworn at by someone with a drink problem who shouts at you, 'You can bugger off. I can say my own prayers!' It may be faithfully praying for someone, day after day, through good times and bad, especially when there is little encouragement coming back in the way of a dramatic change in life or situation. Living with the uncertainty, trying to maintain the feeling of hope and expectation, trying to trust God in the absence of obvious answers to prayer exacts its own price.

In all this, Paul's example is meant to encourage us! He knew that his commitment to the Colossians was never going to be without hard knocks. Yet he saw the afflictions as a strange reflection of the sufferings of Christ. And that way of looking at them gave him strength to rejoice in them, just as a parent at a wedding or a graduation day thinks back over the years with a damp hanky and a lump in the throat and says, 'It was worth every bit of it after all.'

Lord Jesus Christ,
head of the Church,
thank you for all the pains you endured to bring your
　　new creation to life.
Thank you for all who have been willing to bear in
　　their bodies the marks of suffering.
May I know your strength in my weakness. Amen.

Making it plain – Colossians 1.25-28

Warning and suffering are a part of service but they need to be complemented by something more constructive. In the previous section Paul says that he fills up the sufferings of Christ but in these verses he 'fills up the word of God'. This literal translation is hardly English and that's why modern versions say something like 'present the word of God in its fullness' (NIV), or 'make it fully known' (NRSV), 'fully declare' (JBP), or 'deliver his message in full' (NEB).[1] Paul wants to make sure that the Colossians know everything they can about Christ. This is the key to his being able to 'present' them to God as mature people in Christ.

We can fall into the trap of thinking that it is only ordained ministers who are called to preach and teach, but teaching the faith is not something that should be done only by the professionals. The Christian faith has a real content to it. It is not just a few blessed thoughts off a calendar and some fuzzy feelings.

Of course this involves using words. This means that the first requirement for anyone who wants to help another Christian on the path of discipleship is probably a working and practical knowledge of the Scriptures. We get the impression that previous generations knew their faith better than we do. I don't know whether that's entirely true but regular Sunday schools and learning the catechism by heart ensured that they were equipped to answer questions more confidently than we are. Churchgoers often remark on how Jehovah's Witnesses can quote chapter and verse and leave them looking inadequate and embarrassed. 'They seem to know their stuff.' Questions on the Bible or the Christian faith on TV programmes like *University Challenge* often expose an appalling ignorance of even the most basic information. Those who want to help others need to commit themselves to serious work.

The fact that you are reading a book like this is encouraging because it shows that you are prepared to do just that. And there's no lack of resources to help us do it – material published by the Bible Society, Scripture Union, Bible Reading Fellowship, and literally hundreds of books, tapes and videos on the shelves of a good Christian bookshop. Many people find it easier to learn by discussion in a group – the *Emmaus* course is one of several that work within that pattern. And if it's sometimes difficult to find time to read, then it's easy enough to buy Bible reading tapes for in-car listening.

The point of all this activity is not to produce people who are good at pub quizzes. The person who is a walking Bible encyclopedia with a verse for every occasion is often a pain. In any case, as Martin Luther said, 'we go to the cradle for the baby'. Knowing the Scriptures is only important if it helps us to see Jesus more clearly and know him more intimately. Paul says that it is in Christ that we find all the glorious riches. Mere knowledge of the Bible can be as dry and irrelevant as knowing the names of all the James Bond films in chronological order. Nevertheless, for the last two thousand years Christians have said that they find Christ primarily in the Scriptures.

The next step may seem rather daunting. We need to be comfortable about *talking* about Christ as we experience him in the Scriptures. This kind of comment often reduces churchgoers to blind panic. 'Am I expected to do the minister's job?'

It's important at this point not to make 'teaching Christ' sound as if it were a job only for the very academic or those who are 'good at that sort of thing'. There are many different ways to try, most of them in informal settings. A parent who tells a Bible story at bedtime is doing it. Lending someone a book or a tape can be helpful. Discussing the sermon as you walk home from church will help make sure that the preacher's words don't disappear into a black hole in space. Home groups and Lent groups are formal settings for 'proclaiming Christ', as Paul put it, but so is a friend talking to a friend over a pint, or elevenses in a home. You might find it helpful to work out other possibilities with a group of friends. I don't want to give the impression that people who don't 'teach the faith' to others are failures. On the other hand, we probably need to get beyond the feeling that talking about Christ in a natural way is weird, fanatical, Bible thumping or unBritish.

I want to emphasize this because getting to know Christ better is the key to fulfilled Christian living. Paul says that the secret hidden for ages is now out. Christ in you is your hope of glory. That is why he tries every method and uses 'all wisdom' to communicate the centrality of Christ in the life of faith. As the hymn says, 'Christ is the path and Christ the prize'.[2] These verses breathe a deep desire to do a really good job on the young church. He will never give up on them. The whole direction of his ministry is to present them mature in Christ.

In this respect he reminds me of the mother of the bride at a wedding. Right up to the last moment she fiddles with her daughter's appearance, darting around adjusting the dress, the veil, the flowers, even (in one case known to me) feeding her daughter biscuits so that her make-up didn't get smudged. This is her finest hour. She does everything to ensure that the young woman who walks down the aisle is perfect. Many men feel (and are) quite useless at such moments. Eventually and very reluctantly she will leave the house and go in the car to the church. But she doesn't stop until she has to.

Paul also wants to nourish his charges. He longs for people who know what they believe, who are translating it into prayer, loving action and faithful service of the Lord, who have jumped up and down until what is in their heads has worked its way down to their hearts, who live Christ-centred lives and are confident about sharing their hope of glory with others. To be part of that process is an inestimable privilege; it is one of the most satisfying and rewarding things any Christian can do for someone else.

God of good news,
you have revealed to us in Christ
the riches of your grace
and our hope of glory.
May I find him in the Scriptures,
see him in the faces of friends and strangers,

tell of his goodness in words and actions,
and keep him at the centre of my life. Amen.

An exhausting business – Colossians 1.29–2.3

'For this I toil and struggle with all the energy that he powerfully inspires within me.' Paul suffers for his converts but, even if he were not in prison, he would still work his fingers to the bone for them. The word for 'toil' or 'labour' is one of Paul's favourite words. It's the kind of thing you might say when you were totally exhausted after a hard day digging over the allotment. You might use it for being completely wrung out after a six-hour walk in the scorching heat of a Cretan summer with the temperature in the high 40s. Interestingly, you could also use it for taking a beating.

Here is yet another insight into Paul's motivation. He set himself to present the young Christians at Colossae 'mature' or perfect before God. This was his life's project and he was prepared to work without respite to ensure it was brought to completion. We may think he took it all too far. People sometimes say, 'Religion's all right until it begins to affect your daily life.' One teenager came home from a summer camp excited by his discovery of real faith. His father responded to his enthusiastic account with, 'That'll be nice for you, as long as you don't take it too seriously.'

Paul uses another word in the same phrase as 'toil', which gives us a deeper insight into the way he saw pastoral care. It's translated 'struggle' but literally the word is *agonizomenos* and we can see the English word 'agony' hidden within it. It comes from the world of contests, whether gladiatorial bouts involving weapons or athletic events or hand-to-hand wrestling. *Agonizomenos* suggests something physical, straining every nerve and sinew. At the end of the letter (4.12) Paul will use the word to describe Epaphras wrestling in prayer. Caring for people is a struggle. If you do the job properly you can't expect to end the day without even having broken sweat.

It's worth letting these words 'toil' and 'struggle', and the pictures they evoke, play on our imaginations. Pastoral care will involve loving people in practical and demanding ways. It's been said that in our society LOVE is spelt TIME. That's true but I suspect it was always so. It will mean giving time to folk. It will involve making an effort to check that they're all right. It will almost certainly mean visiting, offering hospitality, making phone calls and sending cards, lending helpful books, taking an interest, remembering the big events coming up in their lives, praying for them regularly, making space to talk explicitly about Christ and how they're getting on in their walk with him. One university lecturer I know, now someone with a significant ministry among students, was nurtured as an undergraduate by a friend who called round once a week to study the Bible with him. Another man, when in his late teens, accompanied his mentor on preaching engagements and learned to preach by listening and later modelling what he heard. Two young women regularly take a group of teenagers to a Christian youth rave-up on Friday evenings. It is claimed that the Christian faith was kept alive in the USSR during the communist period by Russian grandmothers who taught the Bible to their grandchildren in secret. I know of a couple who retired and moved to a little village where they immediately set up a home group and started an evening service at the local Methodist chapel. The important thing is that we ask, 'How can I help someone grow in the faith and come to maturity in Christ?' The answer will be specific to us – but we can be sure it will involve time, effort and probably money.

At this point we may feel a trifle tired and not a little daunted. Does it have to be so hard? Paul takes us into one of the paradoxes of the Christian life. He has said that he labours, toils, strains every fibre of his being, struggles, agonizes, sweats blood but at the same time he is aware that God is not standing at a safe distance watching. Rather he works as well, 'with all the energy that he powerfully inspires within me'.

To the question, 'Well, is it Paul or God?' Paul would answer 'It's both of us.' Paul acts as if everything depended on his efforts. At the same time he acknowledges that everything depends on God. He wouldn't have said that it was 50 per cent him and 50 per cent God. Rather, it was 100 per cent Paul and 100 per cent God. This may seem strange but God's mathematics are inclined to be odd.

Here we meet the mystery of Christian effectiveness. There is a school of thought that has been termed *drainpipe spirituality*. It implies that we do nothing except empty ourselves totally and let the water of God flow through us. We do nothing, God does everything. 'Make me a channel of your peace' comes very close to it. What St Francis wrote, however, is 'Make me an instrument of your peace.' Instruments are involved in action. They get blunted in the course of the work. At the consecration of a bishop the candidate makes all kinds of massive undertakings. He guarantees to exercise authority faithfully, be diligent in prayer, in reading holy Scripture, to fashion his life and that of his household according to the way of Christ, to promote unity, peace and love and so on and so on. We would forgive anyone who said at this point, 'I don't think I read the small print carefully enough.' But, despite the magnitude of the task set before him, at the end of each promise he adds, 'By the help of God, I will.' Christian spirituality assumes that we will get stuck in to the fullest extent of our powers. The good shepherd lays down his life for the sheep. We are not expected to 'lie back and let God'.

And then the miracle happens. Because as we strive with all our energy we discover that God is at work within us with *all his* energy and power. Power is something of a prominent theme in Colossians – but it is God's power at work within us. He energizes us so that we can take on tasks that would otherwise be beyond us. Many people can say, 'I didn't think I could possibly manage the job God was calling me to do. But as I took the first step of faith I found I had resources I could only dream of.'

Once again Paul lays bare his heart. 'I want you to know how much I am struggling for you.' Why? 'So that you may feel guilty?' I don't think so. 'So that you may realize how saintly I am?' I doubt it. 'So that you may know how fierce my commitment to you is?' Yes, possibly. 'So that your hearts may be encouraged.' Yes, that's it! At the end of this section the Colossians begin to realize that Paul cared for them and would never give up on them. Paul would always be there for them. He would work his fingers to the bone for them. They had one person in the world at least who thought they were the best thing since yoghurt-coated raisins, one person who was determined that they would know personally 'all the treasures of wisdom and knowledge' that were hidden in Christ. Knowing all that would certainly straighten their spines and lift their spirits. The passage leaves us with the question, 'Does anyone know that we care about them in that way?' Perhaps it's time to tell them.

Lord, you call me to serve you in your world.
By your power within me, I will.

You call me to give time and care to your people.
By your power within me, I will.

You call me to undertake tasks that seem beyond
   my abilities.
By your power within me, I will.

You call me to encourage others when I feel
   empty inside.

By your power within me, I will.

I will, God being my helper. Amen

Keeping an eye on things – Colossians 2.4-5

This section has taken us beneath the surface of Christian service. We have been privileged to see how Paul approached the question of pastoral care, a difficult enough task at the best of times, but doubly so when undertaken at a distance. At the end of this disclosure passage Paul makes one final appeal.

The old song asks for 'someone to watch over me'. Even far away Paul thinks of himself as with them. If he can't be there in body, then he will be present in spirit. The news from Colossae is pretty good. The church appears to be in good order and standing firm. Morale is high. Paul is encouraged. But that doesn't stop him from keeping a concerned eye on what is going on, trying to anticipate dangers and threats and warning the Christians in case disaster strikes. He is constantly on his guard for them. Standing over them as a protecting presence, watchful and alert, like a mother who keeps the children on the swings within her peripheral vision, or a midfield footballer running back to cover any sudden break from the opposing team.

At the approach to Gateshead on the A1 there stands *The Angel of the North*, Antony Gormley's enormous statue, with vast arms outstretched as if to guard Gateshead from harm. It's strange how many people have commented on the comfort they draw from this statue. It's as if it's a reminder of how much we all need someone to be watchful on our behalf. We all need someone who will phone or email to check that we're OK. We need someone who will wake in the middle of the night with thoughts of us in their mind. *The Angel of the North* reminds us that this is angels' work, God's work really, but a work which he wants to share with us. Being watchful, looking out for people, can be just busybodying interference, of course, but it can also be an expression of genuine love and care. Knowing that someone is worrying about you is quite a compliment. Paul is never far away from the Colossians in his thoughts.

This is why he pleads with the church to keep a clear head and not be fooled by beliefs that may seem attractive and persuasive but will only lead them astray. This is the first clue that the young church might be at risk in some way. Later verses will fill in the details but, for the moment, we have to make do with hints. Paul is overwhelmed by the glorious riches Christians have in Christ. He sees the awful possibility that young and impressionable Christians might throw these away in favour of tawdry rubbish, wrapped in glitzy paper but without value. So he stands guard over their souls, judging beliefs by the truth of Christ, having the courage to point out what is destructive and harmful, risking unpopularity. We too need courage to stand guard over our brothers and sisters and children in Christ. We risk being thought of as interfering, but the faithful friend is not afraid to speak the truth.

Now that we have come to the end of this section we have a blueprint of what pastoral care meant to the apostle Paul. It's a demanding but attractive concept, involving exhorting, suffering, teaching, toiling and watching out for people. It offers us a checklist for our own planning, praying and caring for others. It raises a related question, however, one that is important for our own spiritual health. 'If this is how Paul cared for his fellow Christians, whom do I have who is caring for me in the same way?'

This is the point at which I finished the first draft of this chapter. As I began to edit it, however, I received a comment from the leader of one of the home groups who had been trialling the material. She had produced a parody of Paul's thoughts – which made me smile – and wince.

> I'm writing to let you know how much I care for you and delight in you. I know this because I've evaluated your progress and measured it against my checklist here. There is still so much I want you to know and be sure of but I've put together a seven-point plan to make sure the main things are covered over the next twelve months. I had hoped to visit you last week actually but by the time I'd planned, monitored, evaluated and prepared a survey so I could get some feedback – I didn't have time.
>
> Now, where's my list? What are we having today? Ah, yes, roast beef and Yorkshire puddings. How did they come out last week? Did I put too much flour in? Did they like them? Would they have preferred something else? Perhaps I could plan out a questionnaire while I monitor the potatoes boiling.

Ouch.

When I read this piece I realized that I'd made Paul sound over-organized, mechanical and bound by a rigid system. Nothing could be further from the truth.

We all know that pastoral care by numbers spells the death of any relationship. I'm sure there was a spontaneity about Paul, which was the result of his being filled with the Holy Spirit, who is love, joy and freedom. So my last word had better be: Paul was captivated by Christ, he cared deeply for his brothers and sisters in the faith and he loved them in the power of the Spirit. If these qualities are the foundation of our care for others we won't need to monitor the potatoes.

Almighty God,
you have given us in Christ all the treasures of wisdom
   and knowledge.
Help us to discern those things which are of true worth
and set aside those which draw our hearts away
   from you.
Thank you for all those who have taught us faithfully,
setting a watch over our souls,
fearlessly pointing us to the truth
and helping us see our lives in eternity's light.
Grant that, as they have watched over us,
so we may care for others. Amen.

Guidelines for groups (2)

Sharing together (20 mins)

1. Report back on last week's resolution to tell others that you thanked God for them. How did members get on?

2. Share the group's ideas for the design of a leaflet setting out the gospel in an interesting and relevant way.

3. What were your initial impressions of this week's passage and the study material? If you can, mention one thing you gained and one question you bring.

4. Share a story of when someone looked out for you when you were a child.

Studying together (50 mins)

1. What do you understand by pastoral care? What are the strengths and weaknesses of these images of pastoral care – parent, sculptor, shepherd, drill sergeant, teacher, bank manager, coach, servant, buddy, inspirational hero/heroine, A and E nurse, gardener, midwife?

2. 'In our society, LOVE is spelled TIME.' Work out the practical implications of this.

3. 'Once . . . but now . . . .' What is your faith-story? Picture the story or shape of your life in the form of a journey (like John Bunyan's *The Pilgrim's Progress* with crossroads, detours, companions, ordeals, tasks, opponents, dragons and swamps) or in the form of an island (with mountains, safe havens, trusty friends, uncharted forests, swamps, buried treasure).

4. What does the word 'holy' mean to you? For many people it is not an attractive quality. Why should this be so? To judge by the titles of popular Christian books other qualities – peace, joy, fulfilment, power, victory, purpose – seem to be closer to the heart of modern Christians' aspirations. How do you react to this?

5. 'The main thing is to keep the main thing the main thing.' Imagine you are starting up a new church on a housing estate. Work out your priorities, principles and action plan for the first twelve months. How do you ensure that you focus on the Main Thing?

6. Imagine you are devising a study course or a sermon series on Basic Christianity. You are allowed only seven sessions. What do you include? Resist the temptation to try to get everything in.

7. I have learned to be very wary of the famous prayer of St Ignatius:

   > . . . To give and not to count the cost,
   > to fight and not to heed the wounds,
   > to work and not to seek for rest . . .

   Is it really the will of God that we should deny our humanity and work ourselves into the ground?

   Sheila Cassidy in *Sharing the Darkness* (see Acknowledgements)

Is there a conflict between these words and Paul's picture of pastoral caring?

Praying together (10 mins)

1. You might want to use some of the material prepared by the group from last week's *Taking action together*: activity 3.

2. Reflect on the personal cost to any one of your mentors (or soul friends or parents in the faith or whatever name you want to give them) of nurturing you in discipleship. Take time to thank God for their commitment to you.

3. Choose an image or title of Christ that expresses some aspect of his care for us. Turn it into a sentence prayer. For example, 'Thank you, Lord Jesus, that you are the good shepherd who lays down his life for the sheep'; 'Thank you, Lord Jesus, that you are the resurrection and the life, giving us hope in despair.'

Taking action together (10 mins)

1. Some members may be willing to research and give a short presentation about the Persecuted Church in any country outside Europe. For a list of organizations able to provide information see the section on further reading on pp. 99–100. Is there some practical way in which the group can help?

2. 'You need to hang on. . . .' One way of being disciplined about discipleship is to work out a Rule of Life for yourself. Have a go at drawing up a Rule of Life that relates to church, home, money, work, leisure. What will you try to do every day, once a week, regularly (even if not frequently), once a year? Try to keep it realistic!

3. Try keeping a faith journal for a week. This could be a daily piece of writing or something much simpler. One model suggests that every day you fill in your response to these questions:

> The following event, experience, thought, fear, question, doubt or need was important in my life today.

> The following words of faith or hope were important in my life today. (The words can be from the Bible, a hymn, a creed, another person, or anywhere at all.)

From Roger van Harn, *Pew Rights*, p. 155.

4. The group may want to consider practical ways of caring as a group for particular people in the neighbourhood.

Chapter 3
Reality and Shadows – Colossians 2.6-23

Going back to square one – Colossians 2.6-8

We have had 30 verses with scarcely a hint of a problem. And now we get the sense that something is not quite right. Paul strikes a jarring note. 'See to it that no one takes you captive. . . .' (verse 8) What can he mean? What is going on beneath the surface? And why is he suddenly talking about Christians being taken captive?

As often with a personal letter we have to guess and read between the lines. We try to draw conclusions from a host of hints, winks and nudges. We read Paul's vigorous protest and speculate about what provoked it. Something's going wrong. Whatever can it be?

One thing is certain. Paul tackles the problem, whatever it is, with a clarion call to the young church to return to basics. 'As you . . . have received Christ Jesus the Lord, continue to live your lives in him. . . .' Remember the time when you first heard the truth about Christ. Let that memory set the pattern of your discipleship now. Carry on in that faith; go on walking along that path.

Once Christ was all they needed. They didn't pine for anything or anyone else. They were like someone in love. Lovers say the most preposterous things, they behave in irrational ways, they make wild declarations of devotion. 'Are the stars out tonight? I don't know if it's cloudy or bright, 'cause I only have eyes for you' (Warren/Dubin). They sing this kind of stuff, while their friends wonder if they are certifiably insane. The 'beloved' is the sole topic of conversation. People in love drive everyone else mad.

So Paul says, 'Put Christ at the centre of your life. Like people in love, focus your faith in that intensely personal, passionate, exclusive, total way. Once Christ was all in all; once he was more than enough for you. In that springtime of your faith you will find the model for continuing to follow him now.' Paul piles one image on top of another – you will have roots like a tree planted by the waterside, you will grow tall as a building, you will be strengthened by solid food of the truth and you will overflow with thanksgiving like a vessel that is full of wine.

Paul's exhortation is as relevant today as it was then. The ultimate solution to any assault on our faith is to put Christ back in the central position that he occupied when we first came to real faith. 'As you received the truth about Jesus Christ the Lord, so go on now living in that truth.' The Good News Bible translates the phrase, 'Live in union with him'. Put Christ at the centre as you did in those heady days, before you knew too much, thought too much, talked too much, hesitated too much, calculated too much; before faith turned into a game, worship became routine and membership of the body of Christ became a matter of belonging to a club.

Generous God,
thank you for the gift of your Son Jesus Christ
and for your faithfulness to me from the beginning
   until this day.
Give me grace to keep Christ always at the centre of
   my life,
established on him as a building stands on firm
   foundations;
drawing on him as roots go down deep into the earth;
overflowing with thanksgiving as wine overflows the
   cup. Amen.

The basic principles of this world – Colossians 2.8

Along with this exhortation Paul warns the Colossians against allowing anyone to deflect them from their devotion to Christ. Some scholars think that there were false teachers actually in the church, people who wanted nothing more than to plunder the young community. It is more likely that Paul is speaking about powerful and influential ideas that were around in society, a part of the air the Colossians breathed. His reaction is characteristically robust. No matter how convincing and confident the speakers might be, no matter how exciting and novel their ideas, in Paul's opinion the whole show was empty deceit. Yes, he says, it's a philosophy but it's an empty one. It's a play of shadows; the substance is Christ, he's the real thing. And then he uses an odd phrase – the false teaching is no more than worship of the 'elemental spirits of the universe' or, as another version translates it, 'the basic principles of this world'.

Many suggestions have been made about the meaning of this strange phrase. In its simplest form the word for 'basic principles' – *stoicheia* – means the elements, the building blocks of our universe. For the ancients it referred to the elements of earth, air, fire and water, from which they believed everything had been made. We might want to substitute electrons, neutrons, positrons or even quarks; not to

Reality and Shadows – Colossians 2.6-23

mention the speed of light and gravity. But *stoicheia* can also mean the basic elements of any form of human investigation. For example, in the study of language, *stoicheia* might be the letters of the alphabet or individual words. For music, they might be the notes in the scale; for aesthetics, colours and objects; for chemistry, the periodic table; for astronomy, stars and planets; for biology, random mutation and natural selection; for mathematics, numbers. Every system of human knowledge has its foundation concepts and principles.

Now, although this may be vaguely interesting, we are probably left wondering what possible relevance it can have for us. Before we dismiss Paul, however, it will be useful to see what he says about the basic principles. Perhaps we are closer to that first-century world than we realize.

Paul seems to assume that the basic building blocks of any form of human understanding can *almost take on a life of their own*. The sequence goes something like this: The basic elements become the foundation stones of systems of thought, all with their own experts; they then turn into philosophies that people treat with a respect almost amounting to worship. Then what began as something completely neutral becomes negative, restricting and ultimately enslaving. Behind this process Paul detects unseen powers of evil, hostile to God, powers that are only too glad to see humanity in bondage.

A few examples may help. For instance, the stars and the planets can be studied seriously through the disciplines of astrophysics and astronomy. But they can turn into astrology and the mumbo-jumbo of horoscopes and tarot cards. The belief that stars control our futures gives rise to such pseudo gods and goddesses as Fortune, Destiny, Fate and Lady Luck. Experts appear who will give you secret knowledge at a price.

There are many other examples of how secular ways of thinking can usurp the place of God. The study of nature has produced Mother Nature, a convenient way of referring to natural processes as if they had a will of their own. Unfortunately, the personification of Nature has also led to a grossly materialist philosophy that asserts that nothing exists except natural processes. The New Age movement has turned this into a religion, certainly a deep respect for, and some would say, a worship, of Gaia and the forces of the earth. Paul would have said that both philosophies make the mistake of giving divine status to what is created.

Money is basically a means of exchange, easier than pricing everything in chickens or sheep. The intellectual discipline of economics studies the way money works.

But we also read of mysterious powers called market forces, which appear to be out of control and are associated with the worship of the Almighty Dollar or the Euro. Again, Paul would point out that this is a distorted form of worship and leads to slavery.

Sex is a God-created gift, but it can be turned into a divine power. The experts move in – an army of pundits, film makers and magazine agony aunts. Myths spring up – 'Faithfulness is against Nature – we're not meant to be faithful'; 'Everyone is enjoying the perfect multiple orgasm'. There is not so much difference between the worship (and the slavery) involved in sex as proclaimed by the glossy magazines on the top shelf of the corner shop and its equivalent in Paul's day, the cult of Aphrodite, the goddess of erotic love.

Skin colour is a part of the variety of creation; but the myth of racial superiority and the false creed of a Master Race have enslaved and continue to damage the lives of thousands of people.

Objects, colours and their relationships (an aspect of aesthetics) turn into feng shui. This appears to be no more than a fashionable way of spending money on your living room but, in fact, it draws on a philosophy that teaches that your well-being is at the mercy of unseen forces. Unseen forces can damage your house if it is built in the wrong location; a well-placed mirror can divert evil influences. Don't mow the lawn in case you wake the sleeping dragon. If Paul were alive today he would recognize the same patterns in our world as he attacked in his culture.

In this letter Paul makes three points about the basic elements of the world and the powers associated with them. In Colossians 1, we read that they were all created by Christ and are part of God's good creation. In this passage we discover that they can become objects of worship and be experienced as powers dominating our lives. The philosophies based on them may be empty and false but that doesn't stop them being used by evil forces that do have a real existence. Later in this chapter, Paul will proclaim that, in Christ, they have all been vanquished. But how is the victory to be enjoyed? It is to this question that Paul turns in the next verses.

Almighty God,
through Christ you made all things
and without him nothing exists.
Guard us from every power

that would seek to distort our humanity,
draw us away from your light
or blind our eyes to your truth.
Give us such a firm grasp of our identity in Christ
and such confidence in his love
that we may resist all that wars against the soul.
Through Jesus Christ who is Lord of all
and in all things has the supremacy. Amen.

Christ the conqueror – Colossians 2.9-13

Verses 9-13 are difficult to understand but they may just be the most important verses in the letter. One way of getting to grips with them is to note the number of times the phrases 'in Christ', 'in him' or 'with him' occur. There are six instances in verses 9-13 and one or two more in the verses that follow. Paul's argument turns on these phrases. We can summarize his main idea as: *everything that happened to Christ has happened to you.*

Let's see how that works out. In Christ, Paul says, all the fullness of God lives in bodily form. And in Christ all that fullness has been given to Christians (verse 10). Christians can enjoy all the resources of God, his power and strength, as they remain in Christ. But this means that there is no power or authority in the whole world that can ultimately overwhelm them, since they live *in Christ*.

In verse 11 Paul says that the Colossians were circumcised *in Christ*. This might have surprised the Gentile members of the church but Paul explains that he is not speaking literally. Circumcision of male children was a Jewish ritual, one of the most significant ones. It was a mark of being within the covenant of the chosen people. The sign that someone belonged was cut into the very flesh, sealed by shedding of blood. Paul begins to play with the idea. You too were circumcised, he says, in Christ. It's a violent image. Christ's flesh was stripped off him on the cross, he was marked with blood. Now – *in Christ* (that phrase again) you have been received within the circle of God's people, only, this time, the marks in the flesh and the shedding of blood were done to Christ. This new kind of circumcision is not restricted to males however. Both women and men *in Christ* can know that they belong to the people of God.

A less violent image of marking and signing comes in the Anglican baptism service where the minister signs the candidate with the sign of the cross. The person is marked for life and lives life under the sign of the cross. I know of one bishop who makes the sign (but only on adults, not children!) with his thumbnail so that, while not drawing blood, he at least leaves a mark on the forehead. Our redemption did not come cheap.

In verse 12 Paul reminds his readers that Christ was buried. But then, in a picture of burial, so were they. Baptism was a vivid image of being entombed under the water; it was a little death. Metaphorically they died and went into the tomb *with Christ*. There is an Easter ritual in the Orthodox Church where worshippers physically go under the altar in a re-enactment of dying and being buried with Christ. An important part of Christian experience is realizing that our old life is buried with Christ. It's the 'once . . . but now' sequence that we read about in 1.21-22. Like a corpse, we had nothing – no life, no possessions, no achievements, no virtues. We were naked and dead with him.

This means that everything we have and are is only because 'when you were buried with him in baptism, you were also raised with him through faith in the power of God, who raised him from the dead' (2.12). God gave Christ new life on Easter day and *in Christ* we also rise to a new way of living.

What happened to Christ has happened to you. This is the dynamic of the Christian life. In Christ and with Christ we pass through the experience of dying and rising again. The old has passed and the new creation has come. The secret of Christian living is to be locked on to Christ. This passage indicates just how Christ-centred Christianity is. The focus is on a person, rather than a creed or a cult or a code of conduct. We reflect on all that Christ went through for us, and then place ourselves within those events. *What happened to Christ has happened to you.* Our lives are hidden in Christ.

We can see this worked out in prayers from the Celtic tradition. There are prayers called *lorica* prayers after the Latin for breastplate; you say them when rising from sleep. Christ is put on like a breastplate to shield the person praying throughout the day. The hymn known as 'St Patrick's Breastplate' is one of the best known:

> I bind unto myself today the strong name of the Trinity,
> by invocation of the same, the Three in One, and One
>   in Three.

The person who is praying works through the Christ events. And then, in the middle of the hymn, comes a verse that centres everything on life lived in and with Christ.

Christ be with me, Christ within me, Christ behind me, Christ before me, Christ beside me, Christ to win me, Christ to comfort and restore me; Christ beneath me, Christ above me, Christ in quiet, Christ in danger, Christ in hearts of all that love me, Christ in mouth of friend and stranger.

I bind this day to me for ever,
by power of faith, Christ's incarnation;
his baptism in the Jordan river;
his death on cross for my salvation,
his bursting from the spiced tomb;
his riding up the heavenly way;
his coming at the day of doom:
I bind unto myself today.

From the hymn, 'St Patrick's Breastplate'
translated by Mrs C. F. Alexander[1]

Nailing the accusation – Colossians 2.13-14

There is a danger that we shall get carried away with the words of the hymn. What does the idea of Christ the conqueror mean in practice? How does being 'in' him and 'with' him actually work? The next few verses try to show the relevance of the 'in Christ' language.

In Paul's writings, a picture is never far away. They are some of his most powerful ways of communicating the truth. Here he begins by asking the Colossians to visualize the crucifixion. 'Now', he says, 'imagine a piece of paper containing a long list of all the ways in which you have failed to come up to the mark. In your mind's eye see Christ getting hold of that paper and taking it up to the cross. Now he nails it to the cross and leaves it hanging there. It's out of the way, nailed down, powerless to condemn you any more.'

'The record that stood against us with its legal demands' suggests that Paul was thinking primarily of the Jewish law but we can justifiably extend his idea. There are many ways in which we can feel condemned; we don't need a document to make us feel inadequate. Sometimes the written code is a part of our religion. Many people feel that God is like a resident policeman constantly watching them, noting down failings and pursuing them with a notebook bulging with an ever-increasing list of crimes. Whether this is the result of their childhood upbringing or bad experiences of church, the idea of a God who constantly checks up on you in order to do you down is a long way away from the generous and gracious God we find in Jesus. He loved to tell stories of wandering sons welcomed home, of servants forgiven enormous debts and of workers who did next to no work and yet still received a full wage. This is the Jesus who grabbed the piece of paper with its long list of penalty points and nailed it to his cross.

In Michelangelo's painting, *The Last Judgement*, Saint Bartholomew holds the flayed skin of a sinner. The face on the skin is that of Michelangelo himself. What kind of nightmare was he living that he should see that as his proper end? In St Peter's itself stands his *pietà*, the dead body of Jesus cradled in Mary's arms. It is a beautiful sculpture. Was Michelangelo unable to relate the Christ who died for him to the tortured soul who awaited the day of wrath with such foreboding? Sadly, it's not difficult to find Christians who seem driven by duty and consumed by guilt. Why is it so difficult to believe that God loves us to distraction?

This might seem as if it were only religious people who had hang-ups about guilt. People who never go near a church may still know exactly what is meant by 'the writing that stands against us'. Sometimes the condemning voices come from within; we recognize them as the voices of parents, teachers, employers. They say pretty much the same thing: 'You're no good, you'll never make anything of yourself, basically you're a loser.' Sometimes they're the voices of advertisements: 'You don't look good, you wear the wrong clothes, you drive the wrong car, you drink the wrong drinks. Why don't you have a larger salary and a bigger house?' Apparently, vast numbers of people hate their body image and would want drastically to change how they look. Sometimes the accusing voices come from the memory; people recall times when they have behaved shabbily, let friends or family down, betrayed by words or by silence. Some years ago I met a young woman who was almost unable to live with herself because she had allowed herself to have an abortion. Another blamed herself for her father's suicide. Did you know that Frank Sinatra's 'My Way' is one of the most popular songs played at funerals? In practice, however, it's a lucky person who can echo the words – 'Regrets, I've had a few, but then again, too few to mention . . .'[2]

There are different ways of handling these feelings. You can live feeling vaguely dissatisfied with yourself. You can be burdened with or driven by guilt. You can deny that there's anything wrong, shrugging off uncomfortable feelings and trying much too hard to appear normal. A healthier way to handle them, however, is to find the ability to look honestly at who you are and the way you feel, acknowledging mistakes and weaknesses but not being overwhelmed by them. On the cross, Christ didn't pretend that humanity had no dark side, in fact, he endured the consequences of human sin. Despite that, however, he continued (and continues) to love us through those consequences. Our security lies, not in pretending that nothing's wrong, but in accepting our shortcomings and knowing that, despite what we are, nothing can separate us from the love of God.

In the sixties, Cilla Black issued a hit single, which stayed at the top of the charts for many weeks. The title was, 'Anyone Who Had a Heart' (by Bacharach and David). On Good Friday that year I was driving past a church in East London. Outside the church hung an enormous poster of a crucified Christ, more than twice life size. Across the poster were the words: 'Anyone who had a heart could look at me and know that I love you.' The crucifixion is the statement that God wipes the slate clean and gives us freedom to live with ourselves.

Father,
I hear the voices of accusation
rejoicing in the record that stands against me,
sometimes so insistent
that I can scarcely hear your voice.
Voices of childhood, criticizing weakness and failure;
voices of religion, demanding impossible standards
    and distorting your face;
voices of memory, recalling petty betrayals, destructive
    words and guilty silences;
voices of society, disparaging lifestyle, body image
    and achievements.
Against all such voices let me hear Christ's voice:
'It is finished. Today you shall be with me in paradise.'
Amen.

Celebrating the triumph – Colossians 2.15

Paul's second powerful picture is drawn from public relations exercises undertaken by Roman generals who wished to advertise their military successes. The most effective way of showing the populace that you had been victorious was to stage a triumph. This consisted of riding through the streets, making a public display of prisoners and booty captured in the campaigns. As the procession trailed by, the spectators could see what a victory in far-off Germany or Britain really meant. Cheering, chanting, hats in the air, ticker tape from the office blocks, the open-topped bus with the players holding the cup aloft, it doesn't take much imagination for us to catch the atmosphere of the triumph. One lesson was stamped firmly into the crowd's minds by the sight of the line of bedraggled captives and slaves staggering past. The general had defeated them and their power was utterly broken.

Now, says Paul, that is what has happened in Christ. When Jesus died it seemed as if the powers had triumphed. On Good Friday the forces, authorities and powers did their worst. That was the day the big battalions rolled in and crushed the carpenter from Nazareth. In the crucifixion we see humanity at its nastiest, and politics, religion, big business, hatred, spite, envy, the establishment, mob rule – all were involved in Christ's execution. But that is exactly the way the world is, that's how the powers that rule us work. Good Friday seems to tell us that everything the worldly wise say is true, 'truth comes out of the barrel of a gun', 'you can't beat them', 'nobody loves a loser', 'every man has his price', 'when you're dead you're dead'. As in every other story since the world began, the big powers dish it out and the poor innocent at the receiving end can do nothing but take it.

Except that this story is different. Jesus absorbs all the mistreatment but never lets it make him bitter or vengeful. The powers cannot destroy his love and turn it into hate. He soaks up everything that is thrown at him but never stops loving or forgiving, right up to his last gasp. They think they can destroy his life and finish the tale with a corpse and a memory of what might have been. But they are wrong. On Easter Day the carefully sealed tomb they put him in is broken open and he is risen from the dead. In the end his love is stronger than hate, his life is stronger than death, good is stronger than evil and God is pre-eminent over the powers.

Paul invites the Colossians to see Christ as a triumphant Roman general, riding in glory through the streets. Behind, dragged along in a public spectacle, are not people but all those forces that enslave us, that undermine our confidence and restrict our freedom. There is nothing that can ultimately hold us prisoner because Christ is Lord. The power of the forces that dominate our lives is seen to be broken once we claim a higher allegiance and declare that we will serve only one master, that is Christ.

'Jesus is Lord' was one of the earliest Christian creeds and it gave Christians strength of will to resist evil, to defy tyrants, to fight for justice, to evangelize the world and, in many cases, to die with dignity. The pattern has been repeated down the ages. Not just in the lives of the famous like Martin Luther King, Mother Teresa, Desmond Tutu, but in the lives of millions of ordinary, inconsequential people. They prayed 'Deliver us from evil' and discovered that its ultimate power to enslave was broken. Even the old enemy, death, has no dominion since Christ has died and has been raised from the grave. Jesus said to Pilate, 'You would have no power over me unless it had been given you from above' (John 19.11). Every claim upon us that seems so inescapable and all consuming when we are depressed is provisional and relative in the light of the resurrection.

> Lord of all life and power,
> who through the mighty resurrection of your Son
> overcame the old order of sin and death
> to make all things new in him:
> grant that we, being dead to sin
> and alive to you in Jesus Christ,
> may reign with him in glory;
> to whom with you and the Holy Spirit
> be praise and honour, glory and might,
> now and in all eternity. Amen.
>
> *Common Worship*: Collect for Easter Day

Enjoying the freedom – Colossians 2.16-23

So far we have seen that Christ conquers when we are convinced of his love for us in the cross and give him our allegiance as the only Lord and master in our world. His love is stronger than anything, so how can we feel condemned? His life is stronger than anything, so how can we be enslaved? Paul turns from the liberating truth of Christ the conqueror to have another look at the misleading ideas that threatened to undermine the freedom of the Colossians. We don't know as much as we would like about the false teachings in the city but we can make an educated guess about the kind of ideas that were circulating.

We can be reasonably sure that they represented a claim to offer a superior version of religious practice. This was characterized by a framework of regulations and restrictions. There were rules about what adherents might eat or drink, what holy days, new moon festivals and Sabbaths they ought to observe. Verse 21 specifies a number of *Don'ts*: 'Don't handle this, don't taste that, don't touch the other!' The strong implication is that those who did not observe these regulations and prescriptions had wandered from the straight and narrow and needed to be put right. We can guess that this sort of clear, definite teaching was very attractive to many. You knew where you were, it gave you something to do and set you targets to achieve. The danger of this teaching, as far as Paul was concerned, was that it left the young Christians feeling condemned and disqualified, as if they were not serious contenders when it came to religion or had missed out on some vital ingredient in the life of faith.

Along with what Paul dismisses as 'self-imposed piety, humility, and severe treatment of the body' went the offer of a superior kind of spiritual experience. Verse 18 contains a number of phrases that have taxed translators but perhaps the general drift is clear enough.

'Self-abasement' had become almost a technical term among Jews for fasting and suggests some kind of mortification of the flesh as a physically demanding preparation for worship. 'Worship of angels' is ambiguous but most scholars are inclined to see it as the worship that angels offer to God. In fact, one of the Dead Sea Scrolls contains hymns of praise offered by the angels to God in the heavenly temple. Put these two phrases together with 'dwelling on visions' and we can catch a glimpse of a group confidently asserting that if their way of self-discipline were followed, others would be able to enter Sabbath by Sabbath into mystical union with the angelic hosts praising God in paradise.

Paul has already stated that 'the whole fullness of deity dwells bodily' in Christ. The Colossians 'have come to fullness in him' (2.9-10). They don't need any extra secret wisdom to enable them to get closer to paradise. Not that Paul necessarily objected to mystical experiences in worship. He himself writes about being taken up into the third heaven (2 Corinthians 12.2-4). Rather, his criticism seems to focus on the puffed up, all too human, sense of superiority that disparaged the experience the young Christians had enjoyed up to that moment. Some people in Colossae claimed to have access to the very presence of God by means of their philosophy. A spiritual high was on offer though it would involve considerable self-discipline. Self-abasement was essential to success but if you did submit to this rigorous regime then there was a chance that you might make it all the way to paradise. After all, no pain no gain. We can imagine the Christians being gently patronized: 'What? You've only made it to Level One? You poor things! We can get you right up to the Seventh Level.' We shouldn't minimize the power of these claims; it can be quite intoxicating to be offered something more fulfilling and exciting than you're used to – an advanced syllabus in ecstatic experience.

Reality and Shadows – Colossians 2.6-23

Paul's reaction is uncompromising.

- All this claptrap is a shadow of the truth. Christ is the substance (verse 17).

- When people are led by their own ideas and follow their own fancies, they lose contact with Christ who is the head of all the universe. Like a body, a community is only healthy when it draws its life from the head. There are no alternative sources of spiritual life (verse 19).

- It was precisely this life of restrictive regulations from which Christ freed you in his death and resurrection. How can you possibly go back to it (verse 20)?

- And, in any case, though it may look glossy, trendy and up to date, it is all show and is actually of no value at all in tapping into power for living (verse 23).

In this section of the letter Paul shows how Christ the conqueror is victorious in a third dimension of life. We can sum up his argument in verses 13-23 in this way:

- We stood accused and Christ's love released us from the voices, inside and outside, that condemned us.

- We were enslaved and Christ's life releases us from the forces and powers that threaten to bind us.

- We were despised by those who were trying to mould us in their image and Christ's fullness gave us the confidence to live in freedom.

Paradoxically, the Christian who is firmly holding on to Christ finds perfect freedom in being his slave. This is the good news we have to offer. This is the Christ whom we serve. This is the Lord who can bring freedom to people in our world who are desperate. Haunted by failure, oppressed and bent out of shape by powers and forces they cannot master, slaves to gods that are no gods, in Christ they can find forgiveness, power and freedom. I'm excited by that possibility. I'm excited by him.

Lord of freedom, truth and love,
in a world of competing philosophies
let me hold on to Christ who is the head.
In a world of alternative spiritualities
let me hold on to Christ who is the life.
In a world of alluring shadows
let me hold on to Christ who is reality.
In a world that wants to mould me in its likeness
let me hold on to Christ, who is your image.
Through Christ in whom all your fullness dwells.
Amen.

Guidelines for groups (3)

Sharing together (20 mins)

1. Report back either on your research into the Persecuted Church or the personal faith journal you kept in the preceding week.

2. What were your initial impressions of this week's passage and the study material? If you can, mention one thing you gained and one question you bring.

3. Talk about a time when you were part of a public celebration or a triumph.

4. When did Christ first become real for you? As you think back, what differences do you notice between how you were then and the way you are now? What do you feel about the differences?

Studying together (45 mins)

1. Can you give examples of how things that are neutral in themselves can become idols and take over our lives? What are some of the objects of worship in our society?

2. What, for you, are some of 'the voices of accusation'?

3. *What happened to Christ has happened to you.* Do you find this way of putting the dynamics of the Christian life helpful? What other ways of talking about being a Christian can you think of? Which is your preferred picture?

4. The power of Christ has been experienced 'not just in the lives of the famous but also in the lives of millions of ordinary people'. Can you illustrate this claim?

5. A neighbour says, 'It's scandalous! One person does what they like all their life, shoves in a quick repentance at the end and God forgives them. Another person spends all their life trying to do their best but doesn't seem to get a better deal because of that.' How would you reply?

6. The Roman triumph (described in *Celebrating the triumph*, pp. 53–4) was a good picture for Paul's world but might not work so well in ours. Can you think of a more contemporary analogy?

7. How would you explain to someone who wasn't a Christian the idea that slavery to Christ is perfect freedom?

Taking action together (15 mins)

1. Collect some 'breastplate prayers' in the Celtic tradition. Try writing a prayer for putting on your clothes in the morning. For helpful resources see the section, *Further reading* at the end of this book (pp. 99–100).

2. The chapter mentions three stories Jesus told to illustrate the abundant generosity of God (wandering sons welcomed home, servants forgiven enormous debts, workers who did next to no work and yet still received a full wage). Start the preliminary planning for a time of worship celebrating God's generosity, using music, readings (from Scripture and other sources) and prayers.

Praying together (10 mins)

1. One of the group might be willing to lead a guided meditation on verses 13-14 along the lines suggested in the chapter. Take the words slowly, leaving plenty of silence for the group to think their own thoughts. Use meditative music to create the right atmosphere.

Chapter 4
Christ in Everything – Colossians 3.1–4.1

Living in pictures – Colossians 3.1-4

At the beginning of Colossians 3 we sense that Paul is moving into a new phase. He has tried to show how the false teaching, which seemed so attractive to some of the Colossians, was deficient and inadequate when set up against the truth of Christ. Now it's time to talk about daily living, the practical business of 'walking the walk' as well as 'talking the talk'.

He begins with an overall description of the Christian life. It's as if he said, 'This is the basic principle on which the lifestyle of a follower of Christ is founded – in a minute I'll work out some of what that means in detail.' As so often, he sets out what he wants to say in pictures and images. We ought not to despise the power of pictures to motivate the way we live. It's not sensible to say, 'Well, it's only a picture.' Pictures define and motivate us. If you see yourself as a doormat then you're likely to let people walk on you. If your image of yourself is dizzy and distracted, disorganized, not unlike a headless chicken, then you may well find that life calls the shots and you're always running hard to catch up with yourself. But if you can see yourself as cool, efficient, a domestic goddess about to have your own TV series, then something of yourself as the next Nigella Lawson will rub off on the way you behave.

Paul works with three different pictures. The first is that of *two worlds* or 'Down Here and Up There'. Keep looking up to where Christ is seated in glory, majesty and power. Remember the principle – *everything that happened to Christ has happened to you*. Now, says Paul, Christ was raised from the dead and lives in heaven, where he is seated at the right hand of God. You still walk around on the earth, with your feet securely on the pavement. But keep your mind and your heart on the world upstairs where Christ is. Some people wear a cord bracelet with the letters WWJD on it. The letters stand for *What would Jesus do?* This is an example of what Paul means. Keep looking up to Christ in glory. Don't let your eyes and your desires be determined by the values and attitudes of the world. Let Christ be the focus of your gaze and the driving force behind your actions. Keep looking up.

The second picture is about *two times* and we could call it 'Now and One Day'. Christ died, says Paul. But it is also true that you died – when you committed yourself to him and this was symbolized when you were baptized. You died – so what happened to you? You were raised to a new life with Christ. Now your new life, the secret you, the real you, is hidden in Christ in God. No one around you can quite sort out the whole story that is you. You have secret and hidden resources that you can draw upon. You march to a different drummer and can hear a tune that is inaudible to the world. Don't minimize the amazing transformation that took place when you died and rose in Christ. One day in the future Christ will return and then the secret life you have in him will be revealed to the world. Meanwhile keep drawing on that secret hidden life, which is always at hand. Let the *Now* feed off the *One Day*.

The third image is about two natures and we could call these 'The Old and the New'. The picture is at its clearest in verse 9 where Paul talks about taking off the old self and putting on the new self. When you became a Christian something profound happened to your nature. The old humanity was transformed into a new person in Christ. Paul was not so blind that he couldn't see that the old humanity constantly tried to reassert itself. But he is convinced that in Christ there is a new creation. 'You are a new person – so live like one', seems to be his argument. You can go on wearing old clothes, if you must, wandering around in tatty old rags that you've been muckspreading in. But it is more fitting to put on the new garments, the elegant ballgown or the dinner jacket, with the jewelled tiara or red cummerbund, with just a hint of Chanel Number 5 or Armani Acqua di Gio.

The verses that follow this section will be intensely practical, but there is always a danger that they will sound just like a list of good advice or, at worst, nagging. In a world that is obsessed with image we are given three images of the new life. Do they set the imagination on fire? Do they possess the power to shape our lives? We are told to look up to the life of heaven when we wonder what we should do. We are to see the heart of our lives, our real centre, hidden within the life of Christ, one day to be revealed. And we are new people. The people we once were, with all our faults, have been taken up into Christ and made new by his life in us. You are not the slave of your desires, or pushed out of shape by the pressures and fashions of the world or, like a cork on the water, tossed about by whatever new trend comes along. You are a child of the King, immortal diamond, a new creation and you face an unimaginably glorious future.

Lord Jesus Christ,
risen Master,
we have been raised with you,
grant that we may seek the things that are above.
Dying Saviour,
we have died with you,
grant that we may know that our lives are hidden with yours in God.
Coming King,
we will be revealed with you at your appearing,
grant that we may live now in the light of the glory to come. Amen.

Living in community – Colossians 3.5-17

When Paul speaks about the life of faith he assumes that you can't manage it on your own. The Christian life is about living with people, about a new community. We need one another in order to grow as Christians. I remember going into a card shop that sold mirrors designed to perk you up on a foggy November morning. Round the rim were stirring messages. One read 'Hello, beautiful'; another 'The best tennis player in the world'; a third 'Go on, give us a smile'. A nice idea but the trouble is, when you look into such a mirror, you know that there isn't really anyone else there. It would help if there were just one other person in the universe who thought you were the best tennis player in the world, but you know there isn't. And who is it telling you that you're beautiful? A manufacturer of funny mirrors. We need other people – real people who will interact with us.

This isn't always thought to be good news. There may be a certain attraction about two for tea, just Jesus and me. We can imagine one of the disciples musing: 'Why he chose Peter I don't know. He's all mouth. Thomas just hawks his doubts and difficulties around with him. Matthew's a traitor. Simon the Zealot wants to beat up Romans all day long and James and John want to beat up everybody. Judas comes from the South – he's got a funny accent and supports Arsenal. Don't know why Jesus chose twelve. Eleven too many, if you want my opinion.'

Nevertheless, the Church is meant to be a new community, different from the world with its communities. By which I doubt if Paul meant that Christians will have longer faces, more furrowed brows, more tightly pursed lips, be given to sharper intakes of breath and more disapproving grunts. Once, in the early days of the Church, somebody said, 'See, how these Christians love one another!' At various times down the centuries the same thing has been said sarcastically but it remains the ideal. Paul writes, 'As God's chosen ones, holy and beloved. . .' (3.12). In twelve verses he sketches out what the new community will be like.

A community that gives in a society that grabs

The section begins with one of Paul's lists. He is fond of these and many of his letters include them. This particular list concentrates on sexual sins (3.5). Put off, he says, just as if you were taking off dirty clothes – extramarital sex, prostitution, immorality, passion, lust, evil desires and greed. Greed may seem the odd one out in the list but the word means 'unrestrained desire', the 'must-have-gotta-have-gotta-have-it-now' attitude that dominates and controls everything a person thinks and does. It's as if the desire is a god to be obeyed at all costs – which is presumably why Paul calls it idolatry. Greed of this kind has its sexual version – people are no more than sexual objects, there to be exploited. It's the driving force behind the office lecher, the predator and the rapist.

It may seem that Paul is just harping on about sex in the disapproving way that the Church has moaned on and on down the centuries. But this list catches the flavour of a culture that takes what it wants without considering the feelings of others. It's the society that grabs rather than gives. In verse 12 Paul sets out a contrasting list – one that fits the community that gives. Put on, like a new set of clothes, compassion, kindness, humility, gentleness and patience. Against unrestrained desire he sets unlimited concern. The first list suggests that people are objects there to be used. The second speaks about people as persons. 'Bear with one another and . . . forgive . . . as the Lord has forgiven you.' Consideration has replaced domination. Verse 17 sums up the difference – 'Whatever you do . . . do everything in the name of the Lord Jesus' as his representatives on earth.

Lord Jesus,
you have set us an example of what it means to
    live in love,
in receiving all who came to you in need,
in eating with those who were on the edges of society,
in caring more for people than for conventions,
in speaking truth whatever the consequences.
May we who are your body here on earth
follow your example

and incarnate your love
that all may see the Word made flesh in us. Amen.

Living in community (continued)

A community that builds up in a society that puts down

A second list of vices introduces the idea of language (3.8-9). Anger, rage, malice, slander and filthy language are primarily offences involving words. 'Do not lie to one another' belongs to the group for the same reason. In a recent episode of the BBC soap *Eastenders* I counted the number of abrasive verbal encounters in thirty minutes. They came to fifteen – in a number of cases more than two people were involved and in one wonderful scene the two matriarchs, Peggy Mitchell and Pauline Fowler, had a stand up shouting match in the Queen Vic, which must have lasted for five minutes. *Eastenders* is based on a culture of confrontation. Everyone is left in no doubt about what other people think of them. The noted churchgoer, Dot Cotton, said to one character, 'If I wanted a companion – which I don't – I could do a lot better than a lecherous old goat like you and a gambler to boot.' My wife, who happened to be walking through our living room at the time, remarked, 'How affirming'.

No doubt Eastenders exaggerates, but its 'realism' reflects something that is recognizably real life. A teacher friend of mine says that she hates going out of the staffroom because she knows that her colleagues will start bitching about her. I read of a youth leader who tried an experimental game with a group of young people. They all had a piece of paper fixed to their backs and were given felt-tipped pens. For five minutes they wandered about writing on each other's backs anything they wanted – provided that it was true and kind. There were a variety of offerings. People wrote things like 'I like your shoes' or 'You make me laugh'. At the end they took off the papers and looked at them. The leader said the results were astonishing. He had never seen so many secret smiles and slightly embarrassed grins – after all, each teenager was reading stuff about themselves that was both true and complimentary. For many this was a highly unusual experience. The session moved into a discussion of how we live in a put-down society that uses words to hurt rather than heal. At the end of the evening the leader noticed just how many folded up their piece of paper and took it away with them.

Being lied to, sworn at or the object of malicious gossip destroys something inside us. The word 'sarcasm' means tearing the flesh. In the new community words are to be used differently. 'Let the word of Christ dwell in you richly' says Paul. In other words, let the good news dominate the way you use words. In a fascinating insight into what worship must have been like, he urges them to teach and admonish one another. Each member of the church had something to offer to the others. Paul doesn't seem to envisage a situation where only one or two people taught the rest. Each member of the community had a personal experience of the gospel that was worth sharing with the others. Each member might be called to 'admonish' the group – an interesting idea involving challenging, advising or even reprimanding. And words were to be used in praise of God as well, in singing psalms, hymns and spiritual songs. Singing praise with grateful hearts would restore the spirit and nourish the community. We would like to know more about the way in which the word of Christ dwelt richly in these groups. Whatever the sentence means, however, it seems to imply that Christians should take on a personal responsibility for letting God speak to them and then be prepared to pass that insight on to others. The words don't envisage a situation where some members sat silent and never said anything, either because they felt they didn't know enough or weren't important enough or were afraid they might look foolish or, conversely, had decided to let someone else do all the work. More important for Paul's point, however, is the fact that in a loving, forbearing and forgiving community, words were to be used to build up rather than put down.

A community that brings together in a society that splits up

The early Christians lived in a world riven by divisions. Paul mentions Jew and Greek, circumcised and uncircumcised, Barbarians and Scythians, slaves and free (3.11). These categories represent only a tiny number of the total. There was no limit to the ways in which you could create in groups and out groups. Greeks, with effortless superiority, referred to everyone who did not speak Greek as *Barbaroi* – because that was what they sounded like. When they opened their mouths 'Ba ba ba ba ba' was what came out. Scythians were technically a tribe that lived on the northern coast of the Black Sea but they had become a byword for being crude, uncultured savages. They were not much different from animals, drank too much and spoke in grunts. Scythians appeared in Greek comedies as the butt of jokes. Like blood brothers to King Kong, they wandered around, knuckles scraping the ground, cursing, swearing, trashing restaurants, abusing waiters and throwing up in doorways. It's possible you may be able to identify some modern equivalents. Against this background, Paul's words are mind blowing. There is no need to make distinctions between Greek, Jew, Barbarian – or even Scythian! Christ is absolutely everything and he is in everybody.

We too live in a world that loves to draw lines between people and put up barriers. Many of these barriers are based on race. The threat of ethnic cleansing in one or another part of the world is never far from the TV screens. But we also divide people on the basis of class, wealth, education, good looks, gender, politics, colour, age, body shape and interests. Paul asks the members of the new community to do the impossible. Put on love, which, like a brooch, holds the garment together. Don't let your church split apart over anything, whether serious differences or storms in teacups. Let the peace of Christ be your umpire or referee. His words challenge us still. Can the church be a model of the unity of Christ? Can it demonstrate a new way of living together? In his commentary on this verse Tom Wright comments: 'When an elderly person is ignored, Christ is ignored. Where a lively teenager is snubbed, he is snubbed.'[1] We can extend the principle. Who is invisible in your church? Do the young speak to the old and the old to the young? Are middle-aged men or women ignored if they're on their own? Does anyone speak to visitors? Are the unmarried and the childless made to feel inadequate on Mothering Sunday? Does everyone shun the man who needs a bath? Are there deep loyalties across the conventional barriers? Can we do the impossible in such a way that the world stands back in awe and says, 'See how these Christians love one another'? Only where the name of Christ is honoured, the word of Christ shared and the peace of Christ allowed to rule can this begin to happen.

Loving Father,
your will is to create a new community
where your name will be hallowed
and your will done on earth as it is in heaven.
We confess that we often frustrate your purpose by
   our hardness of heart,
our pettiness, selfishness, disunity and unwillingness
   to forgive.
Forgive the damage we have done to your name.
Make your Church a place where
the peace of Christ rules in our hearts;
the word of Christ dwells among us richly;
the praise of Christ fills our mouths
and the name of Christ directs our actions. Amen.

Living in households – Colossians 3.18 – 4.1

At verse 18 Paul switches his attention from general principles governing church life to individual groups. All three of the groups he mentions were to be found in the household, the basic living unit in the world of Colossae. The typical household was bigger than the family and might be better compared to our extended family. It would probably contain the married and young unmarried, the widowed and, even in a modest household, perhaps two or three slaves.

Paul sets out what have come to be called *Housecodes*, lists of guidance to the different categories of people who live together. This form of teaching is not something Paul invented. Housecodes are found within a number of religions and philosophies and it seems that many teachers and community leaders took the chance to set out rules for living. But then, we too have our pundits who write in papers and magazines and tell us how family life should be run. This is yet another example of how Christianity worked within the culture rather than opting out of it completely.

Unlike groups that hived off to the desert to set up alternative communities, the church at Colossae is firmly located within the conventional culture of its time. Christians were not anarchists, revolutionaries, dropouts or squatters. But this raises a vitally important question. Will the life of Christian households be markedly different from life lived in neighbouring households? If the people living in a Christian household could display an attractive, alternative way of living then this would possess enormous evangelistic potential. Neighbours might say, 'Well, they're like us in many ways . . . but they're different somehow. I wonder what they've got that we haven't.' If Christians can transform culture while living within it then that speaks volumes for the power of Christ. Of course, the reverse is also true. It won't say much for the gospel if husband and wife are at each other's throats, if children are beaten down or run riot, if those who work in the house are harshly treated. Paul is dealing with a possibility that is pretty much the same in our world. The most convincing evangelistic sermon your neighbour hears might just be the quality of your family life.

In his teaching Paul focuses on the issue of power. All three sets of relationships are about power and how it is wielded and responded to. Institutional power in our society is fairly obviously constrained by such things as regulations, contracts, personnel officers, law courts and tribunals. Power within the household is intimate, subtle, largely unregulated and often not visible except to someone who sits and observes for a long time.

'Power corrupts' is not a proverb we want to hear – at least not in relation to ourselves. I like the story of the wife of a newly consecrated bishop. 'Since you've been made a bishop', she said, 'you seem to think that your every whim must be satisfied. And you've been whimming rather a lot recently.' Power has been defined as 'the ability to get people to do what you want'. This means that it may be difficult to see power being wielded. Those who are theoretically weak may, in fact, be wielding all the power. Think of the various ways that power is exerted in families or the workplace through emotional bribery of one kind or another, through being huffy or miffed, through silence or passive aggression, or through body language. There are few remarks more debilitating than 'Well, if you don't know, then I'm certainly not going to tell you'. The screaming infant can lick his parents into shape within three or four weeks. Advertisers know all about toddler power and the tantrum of the six-year-old at the checkout produces sweets out of thin air. Congregations can shape ministers to their satisfaction within a year or two, ensuring that nothing too radical will be proposed from the pulpit. The marriage bed can be a battlefield, though no one would guess what is going on under the duvet. In the workplace, power is wielded by those who control information or are able to ignore an issue until it gets lost in the minutes. 'I hear what you're saying' can be a way of deflecting unpleasant suggestions. Tutors can destroy students by sarcasm, put-downs or even by pyrotechnically dazzling displays of erudition. Even compliments can be a form of domination, leaving the recipient uneasy and embarrassed or feeling patronized. We can't always see what's going on but power will be a basic element in any situation where people interact with people.

How then does Christianity handle power in the household? It may be useful to remember that the setting of first-century Colossae is not our setting. Children were not important; fathers had power of life and death over them. Wives were like chattels. Slaves were non-persons, just the property of the owner. We need to bear in mind the situation Paul was speaking into and the differences between our world and his before we too easily transfer across. As we look at the teaching he gives and the assumptions he makes we may still catch a glimpse of just how radical and revolutionary his guidance was.

Almighty God, sovereign Lord,
from whom all power derives,
forgive the times when I have misused the power you
    have given me,
when I have used your gifts as if they were my
    personal possession,

> when I have treated people as if they were not made in
>   your image,
> when I have acted as if I were accountable to no one.
> Help me to use power as a wise steward,
> as one who has a master in heaven,
> and as a servant of Jesus Christ,
> to whom all power was given
> yet who emptied himself
> and made himself of no reputation. Amen.

Living in households (continued)

People not objects

First, Paul assumes that those who have no power are still real people and are to be treated as such. Celsus, an early opponent of Christianity, dismissed the new religion because it dealt with 'only slaves, women and little children'. Paul's new community is for the disadvantaged. I remember a young man in Newcastle who had come to faith after a history of failure at school and rejection by respectable society. He said, 'Jesus is for naebodies.' Paul does not address only the male, the adult and the free. In fact, he speaks to children as if they were members of the Church! Even 300 years after this letter was written, fathers still had the right to leave unwanted babies outside the house to die. They were the property of their fathers. Slaves could not marry; they could be flogged to death; if they ran away they were liable to be executed; their evidence in court was accepted only if it had been obtained by torture. The fact that they are addressed as real people is one instance of the change that Paul expects when Christ rules a household. The Christian exercise of power begins when we see people as real persons, with feelings and rights, and not objects to be manipulated.

Duties not powers

It is significant that Paul emphasizes the *obligations* of the powerful, not their opportunities to wield power over others. Husbands are told to love and not be harsh to their wives. They must realize that enforcing their will, something that would have been extremely easy to do, will never produce love and affection. He will needle her and be irritated in return. Fathers are not to provoke or exasperate their children. Harsh treatment will only lead to discouragement. Masters are told to treat slaves with justice. In the Graeco-Roman world this was a ridiculous requirement – on a level with asking people today to treat the television fairly or give the cat its rights. It is an awesome thing to have power over another human being. Paul insists that the important questions are those that deal with one's responsibilities and the proper curbing and control of power. This teaching brings to my mind that moving moment at the Last Supper, on the very night when Jesus was betrayed. 'Knowing that the Father had given all things into his hands, and that he had come from God and was going to God' (the narrative emphasizes his supreme power) Jesus 'got up from the table, took off his outer robe and tied a towel around himself. Then he poured water into a basin and began to wash the disciples' feet' (John 13.3-5).

Lord, rule over our relationships,
at home, among our neighbours, with our friends.
Keep us from the harsh word and the aggressive silence,
from unfair criticism and resentful submission,
from manipulation and emotional blackmail.
Give us courage to speak and act justly,
love that delights to see others grow,
kindness to give with the same measure you give to us,
and grace to admit when we have made mistakes,
through Christ who came among us as one who serves.
Amen.

Living in households (continued)

Freedom not compulsion

What has Paul to say to the weaker partner in power relationships? He does not try to abolish the conventional setting in which power is exercised but he does hope to transform it. Do everything 'in the Lord' is his watchword. There are seven references to 'the Lord'. When people keep their eyes on Christ and live their lives under his gaze the situation is changed. When we concentrate on contracts, demand our rights, insist on what is in the small print, then relationships start to run into trouble. Here wives are told to submit to their husbands – 'as is fitting in the Lord'. But they do so freely, focusing on Christ rather than being cowed into fearful submission by fear of the husband or aggressively insisting on fighting him every step of the way. Children are told to obey parents because it pleases the Lord. No one is compelling them. Obedience is freely given. The person giving it does so out of loyalty to Christ, not under compulsion. Slaves obey the master out of reverence for Christ.

What Paul is doing here is transforming powerlessness. In a context where wives, children and slaves had very little real power he assumes they will remain free. In a world where husbands, fathers and slave owners had enormous power he assumes that it is still possible for the weaker partner to respond creatively and with dignity. Of course, he hopes that on both sides of the power divide Christ will be the shaping and directing force, but presumably many people were living and working in situations where they seemed to have very little liberty. Paul implies that they can maintain their freedom by offering up their motives and their actions to Christ and doing everything 'in the Lord'. The example of Christ goes to the heart of this teaching. Jesus knew utter powerlessness, entirely at Pilate's mercy but not overawed by him, taunted and tortured by the guards but not crushed or corrupted by ill-treatment, pinned down physically to the cross but free to offer forgiveness. From one standpoint he had no room for manoeuvre. But, in this situation of enforced weakness, he remained the absolutely free person. They could do nothing to enslave him. There can be very few people who never find themselves obliged to do things they don't want to do. This model of handling powerlessness can transform our behaviour, turning something ugly and distorting into a sacrifice of praise.

Order not chaos

Paul takes good order seriously. We might feel that something of Jesus' radical rejection of the conventions of his society has been lost in Paul's advice. But in his own way Paul is setting out ways of living together that will transform the structures of his world, if only the Christians will follow them. If both parties do what he urges then harmonious relationships will result. Paul is opposed to centrifugal marriages, splitting apart because each party is determined to have his or her own way. He is opposed to families where children are unhappy either because they rule the roost or because they are browbeaten and broken down by harsh parenting. Where slaves are rebellious, the household is turned upside down. Where masters are tyrannical, the weak are crushed. There is a proper place for authority and power. When it is exercised as if it were not a precious (and dangerous) gift from God, then tyranny results. When you rebel against proper authority then you rebel against God. But, equally, when you *refuse* to exercise it because you think that order is not much better than slavery, then you fail to take on the role God has given you.

How much of this teaching can we take on as it stands? I've already hinted that our social structures and conventions are markedly different from those of Paul. That must make a difference to what we do with these verses. Relationships between married couples are nothing like those of the first century. We no longer see women as weaker creatures, emotionally, morally, intellectually or spiritually. Children are not property. Largely because of Christianity, we acknowledge their intrinsic worth and don't see them as growing into value with increasing age. We have also invented that strange phenomenon called adolescence. Slavery, with the assumptions and practices of the first century, is not part of most people's experience – at least not in Britain. Employers cannot line up with the masters of Colossae without also noting many significant differences. If you disagree, try branding 'Timewaster' or 'Moaner' on the forehead of someone you work with. Now it might seem as if I am saying that this section of the letter is of purely historical interest. I am not. We should not jettison the material. The principles set out above, if taken seriously, would transform the way we live together, whether in the family, in friendships, in house groups, in church meetings or in the workplace. When people see Christians handling power responsibly, they start to take the gospel seriously.

Lord, help us to do our work wholeheartedly
as serving you.
Remind us daily that
people are not doormats to be walked over;
nor pawns to be pushed around;
nor mushrooms to be kept in the dark.

From favouritism and bullying;
from passing the buck and concealing the evidence;
from the joke that crushes the vulnerable
and the flattery that serves our ends;
from the unjust control of information;
from the gossip that destroys reputations;
from hidden agendas and double-dealing,
good Lord, deliver us. Amen.

Christ in Everything – Colossians 3.1–4.1

Guidelines for groups (4)

Sharing together (20 mins)

1. What were your initial impressions of this week's passage and the study material? If you can, mention one thing you gained and one question you bring.

2. List some of the people over whom you have power and some who have power over you. If power is 'the ability to get other people to do what you want', in what different ways is that power exercised?

3. Talk about a situation when you seemed to have little power or room for manoeuvre. How did you handle it? How did you feel?

Studying together (45 mins)

1. How helpful do you find the three images of Down Here/Up There, Now/One Day and Old/New in the actual practice of the Christian faith? As Paul uses them they are pictures of ourselves. In the chapter, three other self images are mentioned: doormat, headless chicken and domestic goddess. What images of yourself do you consciously (or more likely, unthinkingly) employ in daily living?

2. What images of the self, drawn from the Christian tradition, fire your imagination and help you live your life? (Returning prodigal? Lost sheep? Royal priesthood? Child of God?) Are you aware of any damaging images of the self, whether drawn from the Christian tradition or from contemporary society?

3. Think of one remark overheard in a church setting guaranteed to cause maximum disunity.

   Discuss the worst comment you can make when someone shares a problem or a joy or an answer to prayer. (These questions are largely for fun!)

4. Imagine a newcomer comes into a church or a house group. Divide into groups of three or four and role play:

> a wildly insensitive way of making them feel as if they don't belong and are part of the out group;

> a subtle way of achieving the same result;

> a positive but non-patronizing way of making them feel as if they belong.

5. Discuss the variety of different ways in which power can be exercised in a family or in a church.

6. Talk about a time when you could have exercised power destructively (and didn't); and a time when you freely accepted another person's authority and the power that went with it without moaning or griping (even though it was difficult to do so).

Taking action together (15 mins)

1. To what extent is Paul's vision of the word of Christ dwelling richly in a group a practical possibility? What relevance does it have to the way a house group might run? What does it say to the silent members and the talkative ones? Can people really teach and admonish each other without giving offence? How do you assess your own house group in the light of his comments in verses 15 and 16? Draw up *Ten Golden Principles for Healthy Groups*.

2. Who are the invisible people in church? What can the group do practically to overcome this problem?

Praying together (10 mins)

1. For your time of prayer and worship this week use the 'breastplate prayers' from last week's *Taking action together* section, combined with the material on the generosity of God (activity 2).

2. In a period of silence, think of a real person with whom you have a lot to do. What are their needs, gifts, foibles and faults? How could you do something about meeting their needs? Spend time rejoicing in their gifts. In your imagination, practise putting up with their foibles and irritating habits. Forgive the faults. (Based on 3.12-13.)

Chapter 5
Talking for the Kingdom – Colossians 4.2-18

Being a missionary congregation – Colossians 4.2-6

The last section of the letter is full of personal comments – greetings, good wishes, catch-up time over news, encouragements to stick in and hold on and not drop out. It's Paul at his most attractive, like a sheepdog rushing around checking on everybody and gently joshing them along. Sometimes the encouragements come in such short sentences that they leave us slightly breathless. 'Do this, do that, don't do that, refrain from that, always make sure you do this.' Bear with him. He cares – and cares deeply for the church.

So he begins with some helpful comments about the mission of the church and sets out a staccato six-point plan for any Christian congregation that wants to take mission seriously.

First, nothing worth talking about will ever happen without being supported and grounded in persistent prayer. Sometimes I have been involved in missions, Good News weeks or festivals that have been based on very attractive and arresting programmes of events. At the end of the week, however, the organizing group has often reflected that, though every event seemed to go really well and though the numbers were respectable, yet no long-term effect on the church's life has been discernible. Six months after the mission it is as if it had never taken place except for the nostalgic memories of some of those at the heart of the activity. Paul puts the emphasis not on programmes or events but on persistent, faithful prayer. Devote yourselves to prayer, he urges, using a word that means 'be busily engaged in'. This implies regular prayer undertaken with serious intent.

And pray with your eyes open. 'Being watchful' is a word associated with watching for the coming of the Lord Jesus. It implies prayer that keeps awake and evaluates everything in the light of Christ's return. Don't be a dozy Christian. Pray hard and pray with your eyes fixed on the return of Christ. This will make sure that your prayers are focused on the right thing. People often lose sight of why the church wants to be engaged in mission at all. 'Why are we in St Derelictus having this week of outreach?' Ordinary church members get worried and tense about the idea of talking to the neighbours about their faith. They feel embarrassed and awkward and long for the whole business to be over when they can get back to comfy Sunday services. But prayer and watchfulness remind us that mission is not something we set up. It's us joining God in an activity that he's already involved in. God has been at work in our neighbours' lives before we had any bright ideas about a mission. Prayer seeks God's mind and tries to get in time with his heartbeat. Watchfulness means that everything that happens is seen in the light of Christ and the great fact of the universe – that, in the end, all things will be summed up in him.

That's why the praying always has thanksgiving as part of it. We thank God for what he has done in us and will do in the world and that goes some way to lower the panic level and help us see that God is good and that we have something incredibly precious to share with others. So, says Paul, start the whole process off with prayer and undergird it at every point with prayer and thanksgiving.

Secondly, Paul wants the church at Colossae to be concerned about the whole mission of God and not just their little bit of it. Realizing that mission is God's work will affect the way we see things in two ways.

First, it will stop us narrowing our focus. It is easy for us to be interested in what concerns us. That's understandable and only right and proper. But if our little bit of the picture is the only thing we concentrate on, then we must ask ourselves if it's God's work we're concerned about or just building our own empires. 'Pray for us, too,' Paul says. But Paul was a long way away. Will they pray for him with energy and faithfulness? Do they care that soldiers in the prison where Paul was confined should hear the gospel? The quality of our praying for others engaged in evangelism may be a pointer to our depth of concern for the glory of God. In the Lord's Prayer we pray 'your name be hallowed, your kingdom come, your will be done on earth' or do we just mean 'your name be hallowed in Little Snoddington'?

Seeing mission as God's mission will help in a second way. It will encourage us to be more relaxed about evangelism. The form of Paul's prayer request is worth noting. He asks them to pray for an open door. Well, he is in prison, after all. In such circumstances it would be natural to ask the Colossians to pray for his release. However, it doesn't seem as if that's what praying for an open door means. More likely, Paul wants to be given opportunities to preach the good news *within* his imprisonment. Every situation Paul found himself in was assessed in terms of the opportunities it gave him to further the Christian cause.

We too may find it helpful to think of praying for an open door. If we get tense about the burden of witnessing to our faith, especially in front of disbelieving or embarrassed neighbours, then it may be helpful to place the burden of opening up a way, back on the shoulders of God – where it belongs. It is a burden he's only too glad to accept. Our prayers then take the form of 'O Lord, open a door for me. Deliver me from the desperate need to feel that I've got to engineer an artificial contact point or trick my family, friends or neighbours into conversations neither they nor I am comfortable with.' If God opens a door, then we can be sure it's a door that will swing open easily and naturally. Sometimes our efforts at evangelism resemble hurling ourselves at doors that are padlocked against us. No wonder we fall back bruised and disillusioned. When God opens a door, the opportunities come as if by miracle. Doors swing open on well-oiled hinges. We have nothing to do except walk through.

> Lord, teach me to pray –
> big prayers that take you seriously;
> unfettered prayers that come from my heart;
> honest prayers that say what I really feel;
> thankful prayers that are quick to see your hand at
>   work in my world;
> persistent prayers that never give up on people –
>   or on you;
> longing prayers that want to see your kingdom come;
> prayers that draw me to your heart. Amen.

Being a missionary congregation (continued)

So much for prayer as part of being a missionary congregation. Paul moves on to look at the people the Colossians will meet day by day.

Thirdly, behave sensibly towards non-Christians. 'Conduct yourselves wisely toward outsiders' (verse 5). In Paul's world, life was lived in a goldfish bowl. In the centre of big cities, or high-rise flats, or in suburbia, it may be relatively easy to retreat behind the front door and live our lives out of sight of the neighbours. We get a better picture of what life was like in the cities of Asia Minor if we think of *Eastenders* or a typical English village. In Albert Square or down at 'The Woolpack' everyone knows what is happening. People gain reputations that are difficult to shake off. Grudges (and neighbourly deeds) are remembered, sometimes for years. In Colossae, the members of the church would probably be known as such. They had a responsibility not to scandalize their neighbours or make it more difficult for the gospel to be heard.

Wherever you live it is probably true that more people know you are a Christian than you think. As a teacher, I remember watching the finish of the school cross-country championships. Members of the youth fellowship at the church where I worshipped came in second, seventh and ninth. The head of maths, a colourful and outspoken character, said loudly to no one in particular, 'Hmm, the Christians are doing well today, aren't they?' I had no idea how he could possibly have identified 'the Christians' in the dozens of pupils that he took for maths – but somehow he had discovered who they were. We may think that we are anonymous in the office, at the school gate or walking the dog in the park. But – once more – probably more people know you are a Christian than you think.

If this is so, then Paul's advice is to the point. Behave sensibly towards outsiders. If, in the workplace, you acquire a reputation for being awkward or incapable of keeping a confidence, if you are the last person anyone would ask for a favour, or to help out in a crisis or share the load, then your words about faith, if the opportunity to speak them should ever come, will sound hollow and unconvincing. In the film *What Women Want*[1] the central character acquires the ability to hear what the women who work with him are thinking. It's a devastating gift and potentially self-destroying (because they don't think much of him) until he starts to change his ways. If by some freak accident you acquired such a gift, what do you think your colleagues or neighbours would be thinking when they saw you at work or cleaning the car or off to the shops? And (being sensible and not going off into fantasy land), what would you *like* them to be thinking?

Fourthly, make 'the most of the time' (verse 5). The Greek words literally mean, 'buy up the time'. Paul assumes (this may seem a huge assumption to us) that if you pray, especially for a door to open, then *favourable times* or *opportunities* will come. His advice here seems to be, 'Don't miss them. Have the confidence to use them.' Buying the time suggests that it is a precious commodity. So go out looking for bargains. Get involved in some serious shopping. The word 'opportunity' often means 'God's moment'. It's a helpful idea. There is a right moment when God has prepared the ground. Grab it like a bargain at the sales. Look out for it, get excited by the possibility that it's come on to the market, queue overnight to make sure you're at the front of the line, sell your body parts to get hold of it. The language of the serious shopper may seem strange but it gives us a flavour of how seriously Paul thought of evangelism. What would happen if we gave as much time to looking out for God-given opportunities as we give to hunting for bargains in the sales? The question may seem a bizarre one but it's in line with the metaphor of 'buying up the moment'.

Fifthly, talk to people! (verse 6). The assumptions behind these three words are fascinating and open up a world of possibilities. Paul doesn't seem to think of the Christians as a frightened little huddle of sad people, sheltering within the safe ghetto of the church. He assumes they will be involved in conversations with their neighbours and friends. So he urges the Christians to make sure their contributions to the conversations are full of grace, pleasant and charming. 'Seasoned with salt' can mean witty, though that seems a tall order for anyone for whom being funny doesn't come naturally. More likely, it implies conversation that will not be safe, boring, insipid and bland. Christians will have plenty to say, they will know about the culture, or at least know enough to play an intelligent part in the chat. And they will talk. Paul assumes there will be lively interchanges.

What an attractive picture of the church this gives us. Here are no sad losers fearfully living in their own weird little world, knowing nothing of the latest news, films, TV programmes, football games, music, books and big issues. A journalist once criticized George Carey when he was Archbishop of Canterbury on the grounds that he treated everyone like his Aunt Ethel. That seemed to me at the time (and still does) as one of the biggest compliments you could pay anyone. To be able to talk pleasantly, graciously, without snobbery in an interesting and interested way is a sound basis for the gospel. So talk – in the marketplace, the baths, at the meal table, in the changing room, the pub, the leisure centre, at Stretch and Tone, at the gardening club, the flower arrangers' group, the old time dancing class, the staffroom, on the terraces, at the playgroup and the school gates.

Sixthly, be ready to answer questions as and when they arise (verse 6). Paul assumes that, eventually, questions about your personal faith will arise. After all, you have been praying for a door to open. He implies that you have an obligation to respond. The Greek (literally, to know how it is necessary to answer each one) may also hint that each questioner will need a different kind of answer and that one, pre-packaged stock response will not do. Force-feeding the gospel without regard for the particular situation of the person you're talking to is an insult to their dignity and individuality. God doesn't treat people that way. Neither should we. Different people require different presentations of the good news. This is the beauty of deep involvement in the life of the community. Before the question comes you will probably know a lot about the person asking it, who, in turn, will know a lot about you.

The whole six-point plan takes only 60 words in the original. But if we put it into practice it would revolutionize our churches. Many years ago someone wrote, 'We have the power to evangelize the nation but it is slumbering in the pews of our churches.' Paul's strategy will take serious commitment, of course. We have only to think what faithful prayer means in terms of time and energy. It will also take serious effort to know enough about the faith and to feel comfortable about speaking about it to be able to answer questioners. But nothing of what Paul sets out is beyond us. It is a question of whether we will bother to put it into practice.

> Risen Lord,
> you have given us the task of making disciples of
>   all nations.
> I want to play my part in that commission
> but I shrink at the responsibility.
> Forgive the times when I have behaved insensitively
> towards neighbours, colleagues and friends
> and have brought dishonour on your name.
> Forgive the opportunities missed,
> and the words spoken out of turn.
> Free me from fear, embarrassment and false
>   friendliness.
> Give me gracious speech, genuine interest, practical
>   love;
> make me enthusiastic about my faith and comfortable
>   in speaking of you,
> my master and my friend. Amen.

Nympha's diary

As a light-hearted way of seeing how this might have worked in Colossae, imagine a page from Nympha's diary, based loosely on 4.2-6. Nympha seems to have been a well-to-do woman who was sufficiently prominent to have a church based in her house. In one fateful week she decides to put Paul's advice into practice. Now read on . . .

> Monday: That letter from Paul is really bugging me. There's Epaphras praying, Paul praying, everybody praying. I don't think I do too much serious praying. I've been dozy for far too long. So I'm going to start praying seriously. I've made a start by moving the cockerel to outside my window, with the result that I was up and praying this morning before the rest of the household stirred. And I started with thanksgiving. My prayers have been a shopping

Talking for the Kingdom – Colossians 4.2-18

list so far. I've got so much to thank God for. I don't know if I can keep the new regime going but at least it's a beginning. Let's see what happens.

Tuesday: Second day and managed it all right so still praying. It occurred to me that if I care about God and the gospel, then it's not just my bit in Colossae that's important. So I prayed for Paul this morning, that God would give him an open door. Of course, I'd like that to mean that they'd let him out but it may be better if he just has an open door to preach to the authorities and prison guards. Prayed for the other churches round here – Colossae, Laodicea and the church plant at Hierapolis. And I threw in Archippus and Onesimus as well. Why not?

Wednesday: I've been a bit stupid. Paul said that we should behave sensibly towards non-Christians. I'm afraid my neighbours see the worst side of me. Xanthippe for example. I gave her an earful two weeks ago just because I caught her slave playing knuckle bones outside the front door. And I am inclined to tittle-tattle a bit. Only a bit, mind. I think. I was in the baths last Thursday and heard Kuria talking in the hot pool. 'Oh, that Nympha,' she said. 'If she can moan about someone she will. Got a tongue like a chainsaw.' That's going to stop from now. Anyway, still getting up with the cockcrow and praying. Hard work.

Thursday: Down in the market today. Saw some purple cloth going cheap. Snapped it up like hot cakes. Got 14 cubits of it. Make a really swish cloak and it'll go nicely against my silver brooch. A snip. People desperate for the bargains. Remembered that Paul said we should grab the opportunities God gives us. Grab them while we can. I have a feeling that God has been offering me opportunities to speak about faith but I've not had an eye for the bargain. Keep awake, Nympha.

Friday: Well, now you'll never guess what happened. Had a brilliant natter today with Xanthippe. She seems to have forgotten about the slave business. We talked all the way down to the market and then wandered about and then talked all the way back home. I really like her. And we just chatted – about everything! The prices in the shops, the plays in the theatre, the earthquake in Thyatira . . . . I told her about my plans for the central pond in the courtyard. She's a bit worried about her husband's work – he's in the Treasury. Still praying.

Saturday: You won't believe this! I was talking to Xanthippe about slaves – and happened to say about trying to treat my slaves fairly and justly. She was amazed. And then asked me why I bothered. I found it was dead easy to tell her about Christians – and Jesus – and being brothers and sisters in one body. She asked questions for about 20 minutes about Christianity! I think she's really interested. Wonder if she would come to the meeting in my house Sunday week . . . Hmm.

Well, it's not going to win the Booker Prize. More importantly, is Paul's six-point plan for mission a practical possibility or idle dreaming?

Almighty God,
you have knit together your elect
in one communion and fellowship
   in the mystical body of your Son Christ our Lord:
grant us grace so to follow your blessed saints
in all virtuous and godly living
that we may come to those inexpressible joys
that you have prepared for those who truly love you;
through Jesus Christ your Son our Lord,
who is alive and reigns with you,
in the unity of the Holy Spirit,
one God, now and for ever.

Common Worship: Collect for All Saints' Day

Paul's picture gallery of saints – Colossians 4.7-18

The last verses of Colossians consist of a number of greetings – to and from people that we know relatively little about. It may pose the question: why bother with these final comments? What earthly value have they got for us?

One answer is that these closing remarks give us a vivid sense of the community life of the early Christians. We know a little about some of the people mentioned but, even if we knew nothing, the closing lines still encourage us to work towards the same kind of warm, affectionate friendships that Paul and his colleagues and the church seem to have achieved.

For example, Tychicus is sent to carry the letter to the church and at the same time to bring the Colossians all the news about Paul. Paul had never visited this church. He did not found it – that was Epaphras' achievement. How easy it would have been to assume that the Colossians would not have been particularly concerned about his condition. Paul knows that this is not the case however. He seems to set great store by catching up on the news.

In this, Paul highlights a great truth about mission. People matter more than programmes. We have already seen that the life of the local church is the most powerful evangelistic tool available to us. Knowing about people is the first stage in learning to pray intelligently for them. Knowing them is the beginning of loving them. When a group of people clearly care for each other, then the life of Christ is embodied in them in a way that others find attractive.

This observation raises the awkward question for us: How well do we know the other members of our church? You might like to reckon up the number of people whom you would consider part of your inner circle – you know all kinds of things about them – the appointment they've got at the hospital, how their children are doing at school, how their daughter's baby is getting on, where they hope to go for their holiday. But if you extend the circle, what is the result? How many people in your church do you know the names of? How many do you know by name but couldn't mention one significant fact about them? Even with your close friends, how much do you know about the inside – their deepest hopes and fears? Filling in and catching up is never time wasted, to judge by Paul's letters.

The second value of these personal verses is that they show Paul at his affirming best. Almost everyone is given a label designed to catch the essence of their personality and character and affirm their contribution to the kingdom. As I read these verses I was reminded of John Bunyan's great book, *The Pilgrim's Progress*. You will remember how Bunyan's characters are given names that reveal their personalities – Mr Worldly Wiseman, Pliable, Mr Facing Both Ways, Mr Valiant for Truth. Before you read further, pause for a minute and make up a name for yourself in a similar style. We'll return to this idea at the end of the chapter.

Now, with a little imagination, we can give nicknames to the people Paul mentions. He begins the list with two people who were about to visit Colossae.

Tychicus: Mr Reliable – Colossians 4.7-8

Tychicus is called a 'beloved brother', a 'faithful minister' and a 'fellow servant in the Lord'. Tychicus turns up in Acts 20.4 as a companion of Paul. Some time after this letter reached its destination Paul still seems to be relying on him. 2 Timothy 4.12 mentions that Paul has sent him on some mission or other to Ephesus. Tychicus was one of those thoroughly reliable people who could be counted on to do a job faithfully and efficiently. He will carry the letter to Colossae and not lose it or get diverted on the way. It is possible that he was also charged with carrying other letters to Laodicea and even Hierapolis. The description no doubt warmed Tychicus' heart and straightened his spine. How would anyone feel on hearing themselves described as dear brother, faithful minister and fellow servant? The church is not always good at affirming its servants. Paul raised giving compliments to a fine art. All his thinks were thanks.

Onesimus: Mr Pick Yourself Up – Colossians 4.9

Tychicus does not go alone on the journey. He will be accompanied by Onesimus. In a few words Paul hints at a social revolution. If we read the letter to Philemon and try to read between the lines, we start to form a picture of what might have gone on in Colossae some time before the letter was written.

It seems as if Philemon, a well-to-do Christian, had lost his slave, Onesimus. In fact, it appears that the slave had run away – a capital offence in that culture. Without using too much imagination we can piece together what must have happened. Onesimus fled to the big city, hoping no doubt to hide in its alleyways. There he met Paul – no one knows how – and came to Christ. Now Paul insists on his going back to face the music.

Paul doesn't leave it at that, of course. With a wonderful grasp of what the gospel is all about, he not only sends him back with a covering letter to his master but also begs the church to receive the runaway. After all, he is 'the faithful and beloved brother' – this in a world where slaves were no better than furniture! And he is 'one of you'. There must be no tutting, head shaking and cold shouldering when he arrives. Here we see how deeply the gospel had penetrated Paul's soul. Martin Luther makes a telling comment on the situation: 'This is a right noble, lovely example of Christian love. Here we see how St Paul lays himself out for poor Onesimus . . . . Even as Christ did for us with God the Father, so also does St Paul for Onesimus with Philemon. We are all his Onesimuses, to my thinking.'

But let us not forget Onesimus, who clearly understands that repentance involves restitution. He picks himself up and is prepared to risk his safety in order to 'do what a man's gotta do'. How will Philemon receive him? Paul's letter to Philemon implores the slave owner to receive Onesimus not as a slave but a brother. Tychicus is about to set off for Colossae with Onesimus, carrying that very letter on his journey. Will Onesimus lose his nerve and run off again? Will Philemon do the obvious thing – punish Onesimus severely – or will he break through the conventions and customs of the time and receive him? At this stage no one knows. So spare a thought for Onesimus as he goes back to the very place from which he fled, no doubt gritting his teeth and praying like mad. It's an amazing and moving snapshot of Christ in action in the life of someone who was despised by society, knew he had made a mess of things and who was now determined to get up and make a fresh start.

> God of those who are reliable and of those who
>   run away,
> I need reminding so often that people matter more
>   than programmes,
> try to get it into my head.
> I want to be reliable like Tychicus,
> taking on jobs and performing them efficiently,
> energetic, conscientious, single-minded,
> a model church worker.
> Keep me from leaving a trail of nervous, bruised and
>   disgruntled brothers and sisters behind me.
> And when I get it wrong,
> unlikely though the possibility seems to me,
> give me grace, like Onesimus, to return,
> make amends,
> and seek reconciliation. Amen.

Paul's picture gallery of saints (continued)

Aristarchus, Mark and Jesus Justus: the Heartwarmers – Colossians 4.10-11

'The Heartwarmers' makes them sound like a seventies pop group but Aristarchus, Mark and Jesus Justus form a trio who are noteworthy because they seem to be the only Jewish Christians who have stayed with Paul during his imprisonment. Aristarchus may even have been a fellow prisoner in the literal sense, since some commentators believe that 'fellow prisoner' means more than just making regular visits to the prison to make sure Paul has everything he wants. It's not impossible, therefore, that Archippus too was under arrest. Whether this is so or not, the fact remains that these three Jewish Christians were prepared to be associated with the apostle in the shame and scandal of his imprisonment. They are 'co-workers for the kingdom of God' and their stickability is a great comfort to Paul. This is the only occasion when this particular word for 'comfort' appears in the New Testament but it is common in funeral inscriptions of the time. Paul was in a situation that felt like death and was greatly heartened by the loyalty of those who were Jews like himself. He had had numerous conflicts with Jews; time and again they were the group that stirred up trouble against him with the authorities or the mob. In fact, Aristarchus had experienced something of their hostility when he and Paul were both involved in a riot in the theatre at Ephesus (Acts 19.29). At times Paul must have wondered if all his countrymen had turned against him. Now he finds that three at least were prepared to stand with him in his trial. We all need people like that when we feel like death.

Mark: Mr Comes Good in the End – Colossians 4.10

Mention of 'Mark the cousin of Barnabas' gives these verses an extra edge. When we read Acts 12.12-25 we discover that Mark set out with Paul and Barnabas on the first missionary journey but, for some unknown reason, deserted the party at Perga (Acts 13.13). Paul clearly felt betrayed and wished to have nothing more to do with him. This led to a violent disagreement with Barnabas, which was so damaging to the partnership that they parted company and went their separate ways. Barnabas stayed with cousin Mark, as you might expect; Paul paired up with Silas. As far as we know, they never worked together again. Now, years later, Mark is back at Paul's side and has proved a great comfort to him. We would love to have the story of that reconciliation but, maddeningly, the details are lost. Nevertheless, it is good to see that desertion, betrayal and violent disputes need not be the last word. Conflicts can be resolved in constructive ways. The church is not always good at handling conflict. Mark's presence at Paul's side is an encouragement to work harder at letting the peace of Christ rule in our relationships (Colossians 3.15).

Epaphras: Mr Prayer Warrior – Colossians 4.12-13

Paul had loyal Gentile Christians with him as well as the three Jewish ones. Epaphras reappears; we heard about him last at the beginning of the letter. Colossae was his church. It was his preaching that had founded it. But having started the community off, he does not abandon it. He wrestles in prayer for his fellow Christians, desperately wanting them to stand firm, come to maturity and be filled with everything that is God's will. Once again Paul brings prayer to his readers' notice. Epaphras wrestles in prayer – the word is related to a hand-to-hand struggle and would remind some of his readers of Jacob wrestling with the mysterious antagonist at the brook Jabbok in Genesis 32.22-32. At a critical moment in that struggle, Jacob hangs on to his opponent and cries, 'I will not let you go, unless you bless me.' That is what prayer sometimes feels like. Notice that I am not saying that God is reluctant to bless us and has to be bullied, bashed or bribed. But anyone who has prayed seriously for any length of time knows that it often feels like a wrestling match or like banging on a door at midnight when you are at the end of your resources. Jacob was blessed, his name and character were changed, but he carried the marks of that night struggle with him for the rest of his life. Prayer does not leave us untouched. The word used in Colossians for 'wrestling' is related to the word 'agony' used by St Luke when he describes Jesus' prayer in Gethsemane. One clear message about prayer comes out of this letter. It is hard work, but little of lasting or spiritual value happens without it.

> Loving Lord,
> thank you for those who comfort us when we feel
>   like death,
> thank you for those who fail at first and yet come
>   good in the end,
> thank you for those who agonize in prayer for us.
> Thank you for all who make your grace visible
> by what they do and by who they are. Amen.

Paul's picture gallery of saints (continued)

Luke and Demas: Mr Keeping On and Mr Dropping Out – Colossians 4.14-16

A few more greetings end the letter. Luke 'the beloved physician' wants to be remembered to the church. We know him from his two-volume story of Jesus and the early Church – Luke's Gospel and the Acts of the Apostles. It's strange to see an old friend turn up in an unexpected place, like seeing a member of the family in someone else's photograph album. Then comes the terse phrase 'and Demas greet[s] you'. No affirming description follows. He is the only one of Paul's companions who does not receive some kind of affectionate compliment. Has Paul sensed something about Demas' commitment even at this stage? Perhaps we ought not to read too much into this – except that, in a later letter (2 Timothy 4.10), Paul remarks baldly: 'Demas, in love with this present world, has deserted me.' That's it; that's what he is known for. Like Pontius Pilate, who figures in the Creed only as a way of marking the crucifixion of Jesus, Demas is remembered for leaving Paul at his time of greatest need. In the passage in 2 Timothy, Paul is left virtually alone in prison. Most of his companions are away on errands. He makes a pathetic request for his cloak and his parchments and then comments – 'only Luke is with me'. But what about Demas? 'Demas, in love with this present world, has deserted me.'

Nympha: Superwoman – Colossians 4.15

Because Paul has never visited the church at Colossae he knows few people there. However, one person he does single out. He makes the request, 'Give my greetings to . . . Nympha and the church in her house'. The majority of commentators are convinced that Nympha was one of those able and moderately wealthy women who were pillars in the church. Early copyists had great problems with the name and tried in various ways to change the phrase in order to make it refer to a man – Nymphas. You can almost hear them thinking, 'It can't possibly be a woman.' But women like Nympha were far from unusual in the early church. Women followed Jesus in the Gospels and stood bearing witness at the crucifixion when the men had fled. The angels gave the news of the resurrection first to women, so that they were the first witnesses to the truth that 'Christ is risen from the dead', even while men thought their story was 'idle tales'. In the Acts of the Apostles women play an important part in the story – the Jerusalem Church is based at Mary's house; Philip's daughters are prophetesses; in Thessalonica and Berea 'prominent women' are open to the gospel; at Philippi, Lydia's house seems to be the centre for the Christian community; in Athens, Damaris comes to faith when most of the council of Areopagus ridicule Paul's message; at Ephesus, Priscilla works with her husband to instruct and correct Apollos. We would like to know more about Nympha but the fact that the church met in her household reminds us of the vital role that the ministry of women held within early Christianity. The Church has often been slow to acknowledge the role of women in its life. The doggerel contains an acid truth, however: 'In amongst the noise of battle, in the toil and in the strife, you will find the Christian soldier – represented by his wife.'

Archippus: Mr Finish the Job – Colossians 4.17-18

The letter draws to an end but Paul is not quite finished. He sends a cryptic message to Archippus. 'See that you complete the task that you have received in the Lord.' It would be fascinating to know the inside story of this exhortation. Paul seems to be too tactful to spell out the details for everyone to hear. Clearly, he was sure that Archippus had been given some task or ministry that he had not yet completed. We have no idea why. The form of the message implies that it was well within Archippus' powers to finish the job. Had he lost heart? Or was he feeling tired and needed a nudge? Was the task so daunting that he viewed it with fear and apprehension? Paul gave him the nudge he needed. We don't know what the task was. It's possible that the members of his church did not know either. But the minute the letter was read, they all knew that Archippus had been given a ministry by Christ and needed encouragement to finish the job. If you had been a member of the church, how would you have reacted when you heard Paul's words? And how would you have reacted if you had been Archippus when the bombshell was dropped almost at the very end of the letter?

There is something very moving about these closing greetings and comments. I find myself asking if I recognize myself in any of the pen portraits. Do you get the strong sense that God is saying, 'That's you'? Think back earlier in this chapter to the point at which I asked you to give yourself a brief description. What was the nickname you chose for yourself? Something positive perhaps? Something reasonably self-affirming without excessive bragging, maybe. But, sadly, it's not unlikely that you chose something self-disparaging – Mr Chocolate Teapot, Miss Always Puts My Foot In It, Mrs Lacks All Talent, Mr Miserable As Sin. Paul would not have allowed you to put yourself down in this way. And Paul's Master will not be less generous. At the end of a letter that has focused on the grace of Christ, I imagine him saying to you, 'Faithful friend', 'Valiant for truth', 'Promise keeper', 'Generous giver'.

The fact is that we need each other and Christ is glorified in our different personalities and gifts. All sorts and conditions of people with all sorts and conditions of gifts together evangelize their neighbourhoods. The multi-coloured grace of God is seen in his Church. Our partnership in the gospel is beautiful.

Paul closes his message. At the end we can imagine the apostle taking the pen from his helper and writing the closing words in his own hand. How do you finish such a letter? It has contained a glorious hymn to Christ and a disclosure of Paul's most intimate thoughts. He's set out the secret of the Christian life – *Christ in you, the hope of glory* – and worked out what that might mean in daily living – since *Christ is our life*. He's tried to present clearly the attractiveness of Christ, who is the real thing, against all subtle counterfeits. It's been a passionate appeal to find in Christ everything anyone would ever need. *He is all and in all.*

After all that, how is he to end? Simply – with an appeal and a blessing. 'Remember my chains' and 'Grace be with you'. It is enough.

> Lord Jesus Christ,
> you went up to glory by the way of the cross,
> faithful to death,
> generous in love,
> fulfilling the Father's will;
> give us faithfulness to hold fast the hope we have
>   in you;
> give us generosity to open our homes and hearts
>   to others;
> give us strength to complete the tasks to which you
>   have called us. Amen.

Guidelines for groups (5)

Sharing together (15 mins)

1. What were your initial impressions of this week's passage and the study material? If you can, mention one thing you gained and one question you bring.

2. A lot of this chapter is about good news. Apart from the good news of the gospel, talk about a time when you heard some really good news.

Talking for the Kingdom – Colossians 4.2-18

Studying together (50 mins)

1. How do you feel about the comment, 'More people know you are a Christian than you think'?

2. Are you comfortable with the idea of talking to your friends or neighbours about your faith? Have you had experiences of a door opening in the way this chapter describes?

3. 'Behave sensibly towards non-Christians.' How do you think non-Christians view the church? In your imagination put yourselves in the shoes of those who do not believe. What irritates you most about Christians? And what do you find most attractive? Work this out in the form of a role play interview with one person playing the part of an interviewer and the other an 'identikit' non-Christian.

4. Some traditions within Christianity have viewed the world and its culture as dangerous and potentially destructive. They have counselled Christians to have as little to do with contemporary culture as possible. Other traditions have encouraged Christians to get involved in every aspect of culture. Where do you stand on the issue? What aspects of contemporary life, if any, do you see as dangerous and to be avoided?

5. Which of the various personalities epitomized in these verses do you find in yourself? For example, are you Archippus summoned to finish a task that God has called you to do? Or Onesimus going back into a difficult situation? Or Tychicus, solid and dependable, with the possibility of being sent on more errands for the gospel?

6. Why is prayer described as wrestling and why is it such hard work? What do you find most difficult and most rewarding about prayer?

Taking action together (15 mins)

1. 'Is Paul's six-point plan for mission a practical possibility or idle dreaming?' You might like to commit yourselves as a group to following Paul's 'checklist' for the next six months, with regular meetings for reporting back, encouraging one another, praying and rejoicing together.

2. 'Nothing of what Paul sets out is beyond us. It is a question of whether we will bother to put it into practice.' How fair is this comment? Make practical suggestions about how those who shrink from evangelism or are lukewarm about the prospect can recover their passion and enthusiasm. If the principle 'People matter more than programmes' is true, how will that affect the way we do evangelism?

3. How well do you know other members of your church? Resolve as a group to encourage each other to increase the circle of those you know.

Praying together (10 mins)

1. Paul often captured the essence of his companions with two-word compliments like 'dear brother', 'faithful servant', etc. Spend some time writing down two-word descriptions of other members of the group. (It may be best to write these on separate pieces of paper which the leader can collect.) Use these descriptions as the basis of prayer together.

2. Take one thought that has made an impression on you over the weeks you have been studying Colossians. Turn that thought into a prayer that you can pray as part of a closing act of worship.

 # Liturgical Resources

This section suggests ways of incorporating the study material into the Ministry of the Word as the congregation gathers on Sundays or during the week. A short series of sermons is envisaged, one for each chapter.

I have provided a table of readings and very brief comments linked to material in the Church of England's *Common Worship* for use if you are using the material in Ordinary Time, or if you are able to adapt the lectionary provision for your own church.

There are few suggestions for music because of the variety of sources used by different churches. Though many books of hymns and songs contain scriptural indices, most of the references to Colossians make only tenuous links with the letter and are based on common themes rather than specific verses or passages. A few hymns and songs express a slightly closer connection, of which the best known are as follows:

'May the mind of Christ my Saviour' (Katie Wilkinson) is based partly on Colossians 3.14-16 and 'Rejoice, rejoice, Christ is in you, the hope of glory in our hearts' (Graham Kendrick) echoes Colossians 1.27. 'Praise be to Christ in whom we see the image of the Father shown' (Timothy Dudley-Smith) is a close rendering of 1.15-20. 'Oh, the mercy of God, the glory of grace' (Geoff Bullock) uses 1.15, 'to the praise of his glorious grace', as its chorus.[1]

Passages from Colossians may found in different sections of *Common Worship* material and other recently published liturgical resource books.

For example,
Common Worship: Daily Prayer (Church House Publishing, 2002) has two versions of the Song of Redemption (Colossians 1.13-18a, 19-20a) on pages 553 and 554. This is also printed in the main *Common Worship* volume on page 793.

An introduction to the Peace based on Colossians 3.14-15 can be found on page 326 of *Common Worship*.

In *New Patterns for Worship* (Church House Publishing, 2002) a Blessing based on Colossians 1.13 can be found on page 306; two Thanksgivings based on

1.15-18 with responses on pages 241–243; and Acclamations with responses based on Colossians 3.16-17 on page 67.

Chapter 1: Plenty to Shout About – Colossians 1.1-20

The Ministry of the Word

Isaiah 55.1-13
Psalm 8
Colossians 1.1-20
Matthew 17.1-8

The Old Testament reading is a song of confidence in God's power and goodness. It foreshadows the positive tone of the excerpt from Colossians. God has been and will continue to be at work through his word. Matthew's account of the transfiguration is a Gospel equivalent of Jesus as the icon of God. Psalm 8 ties together the glory of the world that God has made with the kingly role he has bestowed upon human beings in his love.

The Prayers

At some point in the service it would be appropriate to echo the hymn in praise of the incomparable Christ, which ends the Colossians section. The biblical text might be said as a congregational responsory or incorporated into the blessing.

The intercessions could pick up the theme of thankfulness for the way God has been at work in the lives of the congregation. The prayers 'God of grace and wholeness' and 'Loving Lord', which end the first two sections, could provide a framework for this. Alternatively, the intercessions might follow the fourfold framework of petition – knowing, doing, standing firm, thanking – set out in this chapter of the book.

Chapter 2: Someone to Watch Over You – Colossians 1.21–2.5

The Ministry of the Word

Deuteronomy 11.13-21
Psalm 57

Colossians 1.21 – 2.5
John 17.6-24

The reading from Deuteronomy depicts Moses as someone who cares fiercely for the people God has committed to his charge and shows him warning and teaching them. The excerpt from the High Priestly prayer of Jesus gives an insight into the Good Shepherd's care for the flock. Psalm 57 is a psalm of confidence in God: although the psalmist is surrounded by all kinds of dangers yet he takes refuge in the Lord's faithfulness.

The Prayers

The prayers could explore the theme of those for whom God has made us responsible. This is a proper topic for intercession but it also leads naturally into thanking God for those who have made themselves responsible for us. The intercessions should leave plenty of time for silent reflection and thanksgiving. The service could also take the opportunity to give thanks and pray for ordained ministers.

The prayer beginning 'Lord you call me to serve you in your world' could be the basis for a congregational act of commitment. 'Almighty God, you have given us in Christ all the treasures of wisdom and knowledge' would make an appropriate concluding prayer.

Chapter 3: Reality and Shadows – Colossians 2.6-23

The Ministry of the Word

Isaiah 61.1-4
Psalm 16
Colossians 2.6-23
Luke 10.17-24

Psalm 16 is the testimony of someone who finds security, joy and life because he keeps 'the Lord always before' him. Those who choose another god only multiply sorrows. Isaiah 61 was the passage read by Jesus when setting out his messianic purpose. The Lucan passage illustrates the freedom Christ offers and the victory over evil powers that the seventy experienced when they went out in his name to preach his kingdom. All three passages thus illuminate the theme of Christ the conqueror, which Paul expounds in the Colossians passage.

The Prayers

As a visual focus for the intercessions some of the alternative gods of our culture could be displayed on an OHP or PowerPoint presentation. 'Lord of freedom, truth and love' is a suitable ending for such a time of prayer.

Breastplate prayers could be specially composed for this service and the hymn 'St Patrick's Breastplate' either sung or used as the basis of a meditation on the power and victory of Christ.

Chapter 4: Christ in Everything – Colossians 3.1–4.1

The Ministry of the Word

Proverbs 22.17-29
Psalm 84
Colossians 3.1 – 4.1
Mark 10.35-45

Proverbs 22 contains teaching from an Old Testament sage; it is not unlike a 'housecode'. Mark 10.35-45 centres on the way of Christ – a way of lowly service and practical care. Psalm 84 describes a community centred on God and drawing its life from worship.

The Prayers

The fourfold framework of the peace of Christ, the word of Christ, the praise of Christ and the name of Christ could provide a pattern for intercession. Alternatively, the subheadings of the chapter – a community that gives in a society that grabs; a community that builds up in a society that puts down; a community that brings together in a society that splits up – would also suggest themes for prayer. The topics of the housecode invite meditation, thanksgiving and petition about family life and the world of work.

Chapter 5: Talking for the Kingdom – Colossians 4.2-18

The Ministry of the Word

2 Kings 5.1-14
Psalm 96
Colossians 4.2-18
John 1.35-49

The Old Testament story of Naaman begins with a slave girl speaking about her faith and goes on to show the amazing results of her unselfconscious act of witness. John 1.35-49 similarly demonstrates the effects of the disciples' saying 'come and see'. Psalm 96 also looks towards a time when the people of God will sing a new song in the presence of all the families of the earth.

The Prayers

There are rich themes for prayer in this section: our relationships with friends and neighbours and the opportunities for speaking naturally about our faith; the power of names to demean and disparage others and the power of the 'new names' that God gives us in Christ; knowing one another and helping one another grow in Christ through mutual affirmation. Most of the prayers that end the subsections in the chapter could be used in congregational worship.

Notes

CHAPTER 1
1. T. R. Glover, *The Jesus of History*, SCM Press, 1917.
2. Rebecca Manley Pippert, *Out of the Saltshaker*, InterVarsity Press, 1999.
3. Arthur Michael Ramsey, *God, Christ and the World*, SCM Press, 1969, p. 98.
4. 'We will rock you' is from the carol 'Little Jesus, sweetly sleep'; and 'Lo! Within a manger lies' comes from 'See amid the winter's snow'. Both carols can be found in *Hymns Old and New, New Anglican Edition* published Kevin Mayhew.
5. Steven Croft, *Transforming Communities*, Darton, Longman and Todd, 2002.

CHAPTER 2
1. NIV is the *New International Version* copyright © 1973, 1978, 1984 by the International Bible Society. J. B. Phillips' *The New Testament in Modern English* (JBP), was published by Geoffrey Bles in 1960. NEB is *The New English Bible*, Oxford University Press/Cambridge University Press, 1970.
2. These words are from 'Fight the good fight', which can be found in many hymnbooks.

CHAPTER 3
1. This version of the hymn is in *Hymns Old and New*, Anglican edition, Kevin Mayhew, 1986.
2. 'My Way', by Paul Anka and Frank Sinatra.

CHAPTER 4
1. From p. 140 of *The Epistles of Paul to the Colossians and Philemon*. See *Further Reading* for full details.

CHAPTER 5
1. *What Women Want*, directed by Nancy Meyers, 2000.

LITURGICAL RESOURCES
1. 'May the mind' and Rejoice, rejoice' are both in *Mission Praise*, Marshall Pickering, 1990.
Timothy Dudley-Smith's hymn is found in *Praise! Psalms, hymns and songs for Christian worship*, Praise Trust, 2000.
'Oh the mercy' is in *Worship Today*, published by Spring Harvest.

 # Further Reading

For those who want to explore Colossians further through commentaries either because they are leading groups or preparing sermons, the following books should prove helpful.

N. T. Wright, *The Epistles of Paul to the Colossians and Philemon: an introduction and commentary*, Tyndale New Testament Commentaries, InterVarsity Press and William B. Eerdmans, 1994. This is probably the most accessible commentary not requiring a knowledge of the Greek text.

Peter T. O'Brien, *Colossians, Philemon*, Word Biblical Commentary, Volume 44, Word Books, 1982.

James D. G. Dunn, *The Epistles to the Colossians and to Philemon*, The New International Greek Testament Commentary, Paternoster and Eerdmans, 1996.

O'Brien and Dunn are both superb, surveying in a balanced fashion the variety of views that have been held on all the key issues, yet never forgetting the need of the preacher to get a grasp of Paul's thought.

Eduard Lohse, *A Commentary on the Epistles to the Colossians and to Philemon*, (trans. W. R. Poelmann and R. J. Harris), Fortress Press, 1971. This is one of the volumes in the Hermeneia series and is recognized as a heavyweight commentary. Lohse is especially good on Graeco-Roman culture.

In the course of my reading I came across three wonderful summaries of Colossians, which present the whole argument of the letter in a brief compass. It is easy to get bogged down in the details of Paul's discussions and lose the sense of where he is going. These three treatments help you get an overview of Paul's thought and show how individual sections contribute to an integrated argument. They are buried in longer books but Tom Wright's book is not too long and can be purchased from Christian bookshops and the books by Barclay and Lincoln may be obtained from libraries.

'The battle won: Colossians' in N. T. Wright, *Following Jesus: biblical reflections on discipleship*, SPCK, 1994, pp. 10–18.

'The theology of Colossians' in John M. G. Barclay, *Colossians and Philemon*, New Testament Guides series, Sheffield Academic Press, 1997, pp. 75–96.

'Colossians and heavenly mindedness' in Andrew T. Lincoln, *Paradise now and not yet: studies in the role of the heavenly dimension in Paul's thought with special reference to his eschatology*, Cambridge University Press, 1981, pp. 110–134.

For information on the Persecuted Church (mentioned in 'Taking action together' at the end of Chapter 2) contact any of the following organizations:

Christian Solidarity Worldwide, PO Box 99, New Malden, Surrey, KT3 3YG. Tel: 020 8942 8810. Web site: www.csw.org.uk.

The Barnabas Fund/Institute for the Study of Islam and Christianity, The Old Rectory, River Street, Pewsey, Wiltshire, SN9 5DB. Tel: 01672 564938. Web site: www.barnabasfund.org.

Keston Institute, 4 Park Town, Oxford, OX2 6SH. Tel: 01865 311022. Web site: www.keston.org.

Jubilee Campaign and Jubilee Action, St John's Cranleigh Road, Wonersh, Guildford, Surrey, GU5 0QX. Web site: www.jubileecampaign.demon.co.uk.

Open Doors, PO Box 6, Witney, Oxfordshire, OX8 7SP. Tel: 01865 301300. Web site: www.od.org/oduk.

For examples of Breastplate Prayers (mentioned in 'Taking action together', Chapter 3 p.5) see any of the books of David Adam, all published by SPCK Triangle: *The Edge of Glory* (1985), *The Cry of the Deer* (1987), *The Eye of the Eagle* (1990), *Border Lands* (1991), *Power Lines* (1992), *The Rhythm of Life* (1996). In addition to these books, an Internet search under the key words 'lorica prayers' may produce more examples.

Notes on the Order for Daily Prayer

Christians in every generation have found it helpful to pray and listen to Scripture using a prepared form, sometimes called a Daily Office. A very simple office is provided here for readers of this book who are not used to praying in this way and who want to set their Bible reading in the context of daily prayer.

It is helpful to find a regular time and place each day. Choose the time of day that is most convenient and helpful for you. There are six sections in each chapter and psalms are suggested for the six weekdays. The Preparation begins with a sentence of Scripture, the Song of the Word of the Lord (Isaiah 55.6-11) and an opportunity for quiet prayer.

There are suggested psalms for each day. The psalms chosen reflect different aspects of God's character and our encounter with him. The first set of psalms are intended to be read for three weeks and the second set for the final two weeks. There is then space to read the set Bible passage and the notes.

The prayers are in response to the Word of God. Offer your own prayers of intercession in the place suggested. It may help to keep a short list of people and situations you pray for regularly.

If you find this way of praying helpful, you may want to explore a more developed form of the Daily Office. One example, with a rich variety of material, is *Common Worship: Daily Prayer Preliminary Edition*, Church House Publishing, 2002.

An Order for Daily Prayer

Preparation

You have been raised with Christ,
seek the things that are above.
Set your minds on things that are above,
not on things that are on earth.
For you have died,
and your life is hidden with Christ in God.

(Colossians 3.1-3)

The Song of the Word of the Lord
Seek the Lord while he may be found,
call upon him while he is near;
let the wicked abandon their ways,
and the unrighteous their thoughts;
return to the Lord, who will have mercy;
to our God, who will richly pardon.
'For my thoughts are not your thoughts,
neither are your ways my ways,' says the Lord.
'For as the heavens are higher than the earth,
so are my ways higher than your ways
      and my thoughts than your thoughts.
As the rain and the snow come down from above,
and return not again but water the earth,
bringing forth life and giving growth,
seed for sowing and bread to eat,
so is my word that goes forth from my mouth;
it will not return to me fruitless,
but it will accomplish that which I purpose,
and succeed in the task I gave it.'

(Isaiah 55.6-11)

Opening prayer

Stir up in us, O God, the fire of your love,
that we may be cleansed of all our sins
and so be made ready to come into your presence,
singing your praises now and for ever. Amen.

(From *Celebrating Common Prayer*)

Silence is kept.

Daily psalms

Monday	29	98
Tuesday	8	84
Wednesday	1	119.1-16
Thursday	26	13
Friday	15	24
Saturday	145	34

Bible reading

(using the passage for the day)

Reflection on the Bible reading

Reading the notes

Prayers

The short prayer for the day (from the notes)

Intercessions are offered

The Lord's Prayer

Our Father in heaven,
hallowed be your name,
your kingdom come,
your will be done,
on earth as in heaven.
Give us today our daily bread.
Forgive us our sins
as we forgive those who sin against us.
Lead us not into temptation
but deliver us from evil.
For the kingdom, the power,
and the glory are yours,
now and for ever.
Amen.

Almighty God,
we thank you for the gift of your holy word.
May it be a lantern to our feet,
a light to our paths,
and a strength to our lives.
Take us and use us
to love and serve all people
in the power of the Holy Spirit
and in the name of your Son,
Jesus Christ our Lord.
Amen.

Common Worship: p. 47

If you have enjoyed using this Emmaus Bible Resource, you may be interested in *Emmaus: The Way of Faith*. This resource is designed to help churches welcome people into the Christian faith and the life of the Church.

Emmaus has three stages – contact, nurture and growth. It encourages the vision of the local church for evangelism and gives practical advice on how to develop contact with those outside the Church. The course material provided includes a 15-week nurture course that covers the basics of the Christian life and four growth books that offer Christians an opportunity to deepen their understanding of Christian living and discipleship.

All the group notes are fully photocopiable.

The authors are Stephen Cottrell, Steven Croft, John Finney, Felicity Lawson, Robert Warren.

Visit our web site www.e-mmaus.org.uk, email any enquiries to: emmaus@c-of-e.org.uk or call 020 7898 1524.

Emmaus: The Way of Faith

Introduction: 2nd edition
£4.95   0 7151 4963 6
Essential background to both the theology and practice of Emmaus and includes material on how to run the course in your own church.

Leading an Emmaus Group

£5.95   0 7151 4905 9
Straightforward and direct guide to leading both Nurture and Growth groups. It lays a biblical framework for group leadership, using Jesus as the example and model.

Contact: 2nd Edition

£5.95   0 7151 4995 4
Explores ways that your church can be involved in evangelism and outreach and make contact with those outside the Church.

Nurture: 2nd Edition

£22.50   0 7151 4994 6
A 15-session course covering the basics of Christian life and faith.

Growth: Knowing God

£17.50   0 7151 4875 3
Four short courses for growing Christians: Living the Gospel; Knowing the Father; Knowing Jesus; and Come, Holy Spirit.

Growth: Growing as a Christian

£17.50   0 7151 4876 1
Five short courses for growing Christians: Growing in Prayer; Growing in the Scriptures; Being Church; Growing in Worship; and Life, Death and Christian Hope.

Growth: Christian Lifestyle

£15.00   0 7151 4877 X
Four short courses for growing Christians: Living Images; Overcoming Evil; Personal Identity; and Called into Life.

Growth: Your Kingdom Come

£15.00   0 7151 4904 0
This Growth book looks in depth at two main issues: the Beatitudes and the Kingdom.

Youth Emmaus

£19.95   0 7151 4988 1
Aimed specifically at young people aged 11-16 Youth Emmaus tackles the basics of the Christian faith.

Related Titles

Travelling Well: A Companion Guide to the Christian Faith

Stephen Cottrell and Steven Croft
£6.95   0 7151 4935 0
Provides instruction for important areas in Christian life such as prayer, reading the Bible, worship and relating faith to daily life. Ideal for adult Christians who are beginning the journey of faith.

Emmaus Bible Resources – other titles in the series

Emmaus Bible Resources – Ideal for small groups!

Finding a middle ground between daily Bible notes and weighty commentaries, the series adopts the Emmaus approach of combining sound theology and good educational practice with a commitment to equip the whole Church for mission.

Each book contains leader's guidelines, short prayers or meditations, a commentary, discussion questions and practical 'follow-on' activities.

The Lord is Risen!: Luke 24
Steven Croft
£7.95   0 7151 4971 7

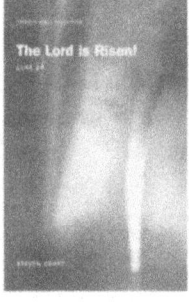

The 50 days from Easter to Pentecost are a unique period in the history of the Christian faith. *The Lord is Risen!* takes us on a journey through Luke that strengthens, challenges, deepens and renews our Christian discipleship. An ideal 'Easter' book.

Missionary Journeys, Missionary Church: Acts 13–20
Steven Croft
£7.95   0 7151 4972 5

The book of Acts is the most exciting and dramatic in the New Testament. Throughout Christian history, men and women have returned to the book of Acts to find their faith and ministry renewed and rekindled.

A Rebellious Prophet: Jonah
Joy Tetley
£7.95   0 7151 4986 5

Prejudiced, petulant, resentful, sulky: Jonah was not just a reluctant spokesman for God, he was also a disobedient one. The story of Jonah shows how God calls and uses those who are far from perfect. As Christians, we are not all called to be prophets. But we are all called to respond in some way to God's prompting. This study of the book of Jonah challenges us to do just that.

Available at all good Christian bookshops or direct on 020 7898 1300 or visit www.chpublishing.co.uk for online purchasing.

ww.ingramcontent.com/pod-product-compliance
htning Source LLC
nbersburg PA
W051952290426
0CB00015B/2212